IMAGES
of America

LINCOLN HEIGHTS

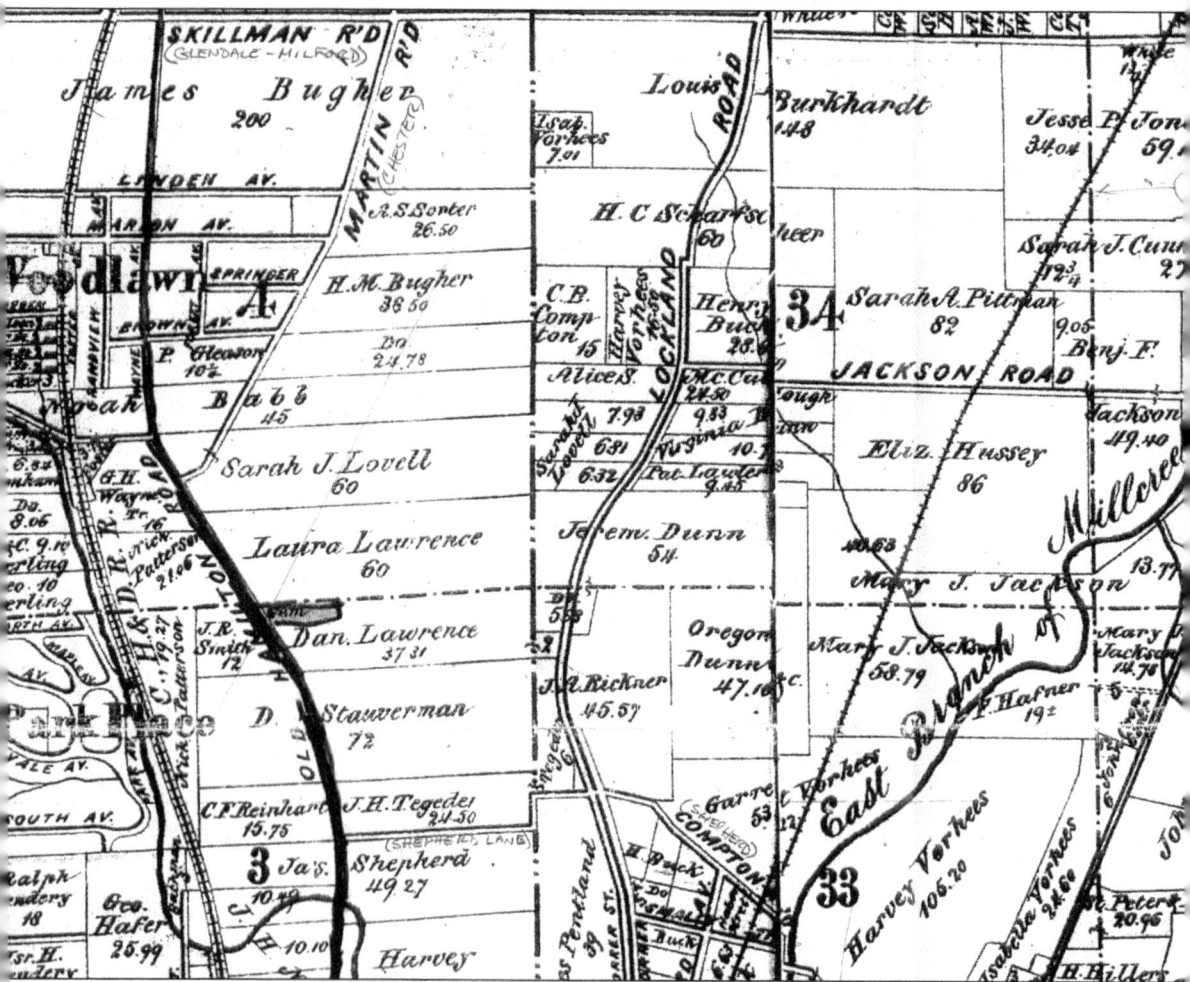

This early 1884 map shows the location of the village of Lincoln Heights, incorporated in 1946, 62 years after the sale of the land from Henry Kuneven to Roy M. Haley. Later that same day, Wallace R. Livingston purchased half interest in Haley's new property. (Courtesy of the Public Library of Cincinnati and Hamilton County.)

On the cover: Held to celebrate the incorporation of Lincoln Heights, the Lincoln Heights Day Festival is fun for everyone in the community. The Lincoln Heights festival 1955 baseball team is seen here. From left to right are (first row) Rev. Prentiss Brown, Willie Lindsay, and Deacon James Gray; (second row) Willie Farrow, Earl Fredericks, Claude West, Rodgers, Bob Barber, Deacon Timothy Holland, Gilbert Lindsay, James McCoy. (Courtesy of Mildred Williams.)

IMAGES
of America

LINCOLN HEIGHTS

Carolyn F. Smith

ARCADIA
PUBLISHING

Published by Arcadia Publishing
Charleston SC, Chicago IL, Portsmouth NH, San Francisco CA

Library of Congress Catalog Card Number: 2008925389

For all general information contact Arcadia Publishing at:
Telephone 843-853-2070
Fax 843-853-0044
E-mail sales@arcadiapublishing.com
For customer service and orders:
Toll-Free 1-888-313-2665

Visit us on the Internet at www.arcadiapublishing.com

To my grandchildren, Lexus McCrary, Alyssa and Grant Smith, and Kennedy Dawson—reach for the universe. For my maternal grandparents Frank and Lois Perry, and to my aunts Treva Perry Thompson and Anna Perry, I love and miss you both.

CONTENTS

Acknowledgments   6

Introduction   7

1.   In the Beginning   9

2.   Hearing God's Words   27

3.   St. Simon of Cyrene   39

4.   Built by the People for the People   55

5.   School Days   79

6.   Food, Fun, and Family   95

7.   People of Lincoln Heights   109

Bibliography   127

ACKNOWLEDGMENTS

To those individuals who are no longer here but had the vision and insight to aspire and do, thank you Rev. Michael Mangham, Cecil Hunter, Guy T. Westmoreland, Eugene Fulton, William Robert Flowers, Marianna Matthews, Magnolia Craig, and all others whose names I have not written down or may have forgotten.

I would like to thank the following individuals who gave me the idea to do this: Dr. Mary Anne Pittman, professor at the University of Cincinnati College of Education, who sparked my interest in the topic by asking the question, "Do you know who you are?" in her cultural diversity class in the graduate division level. I would also like to acknowledge Dr. Leo Krzywkowski, who was my former master thesis advisor at the University of Cincinnati. He always gave me encouraging words and advice. Thanks Dr. K.

I would personally like to acknowledge the following individuals for allowing me to ask a lot of questions and provide me with their precious photographs, because without them there would be no pictures or project: Mildred Lindsay Williams, Winfred Mangham, Andrienne and Harry Howard, Jeannette Crawford, Angela Thompson (who was very helpful in gathering church photographs for me), Richard Lewis, Marietta Roseman, Mollie Mangham Spears (granddaughter of Rev. Mike Mangham), Carol Murden, Allen Harrison, John Key, and Lorene Jones for identifying a lot of the faces in the photographs when no one else could.

To the late William P. Davis and to my mother, Quincy Perry Davis—thank you. To my children Ronald Smith Jr., Kendra Smith Dawson, Michael K. Smith—thanks for understanding when I would say, "I'll call you later." Thank you Joseph Smith for your encouraging words.

INTRODUCTION

The Miami-Erie Canal, which connected Lake Erie with the Ohio River, was constructed through the wide, fertile Mill Creek Valley north of Cincinnati. The barge traffic on the canal carried lumber, iron ore, and asbestos from the north, and a multitude of finished manufactured goods were transported back from Cincinnati to the north. The prosperity and rapid growth of industry in Cincinnati was so dynamic in the early 1900s that many factories began to locate in the Mill Creek Valley along the Miami-Erie Canal.

The events of World War I and the growth of industry in the Mill Creek Valley created a demand for large numbers of black laborers, many coming from the South, to work in the new and expanded factories in the valley. Upon their arrival, blacks found very few living accommodations in the areas of Lockland, Reading, Wyoming, and other places near their jobs. In the early part of the 20th century, Lockland provided the largest number of housing units for blacks. The black district of Lockland was bounded by Washington Avenue in the east, Stewart Avenue in the north, Wyoming Avenue in the south, and the Baltimore and Ohio (B&O) Railroad in the west. A fence was constructed by the City of Lockland on the eastern border of the black neighborhood just a few yards east of Wayne Avenue to stop the black population from straying over into "white" Lockland. The tightly defined, highly populated black district of Lockland became overcrowded, and the often violent and inhumane living conditions created a demand for new living spaces for blacks.

On October 20, 1923, Roy M. Haley purchased land from Henry Kunevens and along with Wallace R. and Katherine Livingston formed the Haley-Livingston Land Company. Their main office was in Chicago, but a branch office was maintained in their new Cincinnati Industrial Subdivision, which consisted of 47.57 acres of land in Springfield Township. M. J. Behles, a white real estate salesman, bought the first lot from the Haley-Livingston Land Company on January 17, 1924. The black families of William and Sadie Gooch and Peter and Allie Finch followed in also purchasing lots. The new community had three-and-a-half streets: Behles, Simmons, Steffens, and half of Schumard. The streets were not paved or graded; there were no curbs, sidewalks, or gutters placed on the streets; there were no easements for utilities or storm water drainage; to maximize land usage, there were no alleys, and no land was set aside for stores, schools, parks, or churches.

On March 28, 1925, Wallace R. Livingston purchased three-and-a-half acres of land for a second subdivision from Katherine M. Kuneven. The newly acquired section, located in Sycamore Township, became the Cincinnati Industrial Subdivision Annex. In the fall of the same year, Doris D. and Edward Rempke also purchased 46 acres located in Sycamore Township from Kuneven. The acquisition was later developed into the third subdivision, Valley View. The majority of Valley View residents were employees of the Tennessee Fertilizer Company.

Washington Subdivision, again located in Sycamore Township, was formed by Haley-Livingston Land Company from lots one, two, and three of the Jeremiah Dunn estate and became the fourth subdivision. In October 1925, the Haley-Livingston Land Company purchased 21.3 acres of land from Addison E. Cole. One-year later, Haley-Livingston purchased another tract of land from Cole. This fifth subdivision was named Oak Park Subdivision.

In early May 1926, Charles W. Steele, an executive with a local trucking company, and his associates formed the Grandview Heights Realty Company. They purchased 55.5 acres of land in the Sycamore Township from Cole. The new subdivision was named Grandview Heights.

On the same day in 1926 that Grandview Heights opened for occupancy, groundwork on a similar community started. The new subdivision was to be named Woodlawn Terrace. It contained 26.19 acres in Springfield Township. From March 3, 1921, until October 6, 1926, there were three different owners. In 1921, Albert Armstrong and his family purchased the land and developed two subdivisions. He released all rights to the property to his relatives, and upon the completion of the new development, the ownership of the land changed again. This time, control of Woodlawn Terrace was under the power of attorney of Albert Armstrong.

James I. Estes, another local businessman, hoped to make a quick profit from real estate sales. He developed a subdivision called the Lincoln Heights Subdivision Annex, located in Sycamore Township. Estes died before any lots were sold, and the court appointed Clara Holthaus as the executive of the estate. Holthaus sold the lots in the Lincoln Heights subdivision.

Daniel Laurence, a member of the old and prominent white Dunn family of the Mill Creek Valley, was concerned with the problem of housing for black families in 1927. He established the seventh living area, Lincoln Heights Subdivision, for blacks working and residing in the valley on August 17, 1927. He developed the area from 37.3 acres of his own land situated in the northeast corner of Springfield Township, property that had been in his family since 1867.

Lincoln Heights incorporated in 1946 as one of the first self-governing African American communities north of the Mason-Dixon Line. Today Lincoln Heights is a very family oriented community. Many residents have either come back home to live in family owned houses, or they never left. For example, Carolyn Carr, former mayor Deborah Seay, Tyrone Mynatt, Robert Carr, Gertha Ann Carr, Carol Murden, Charlotte Kemper, Edith Price, Lois Graham, Roxie Foster, and others are still in the neighborhood today. Lincoln Heights has given its residents the feeling of wealth. They have wealth that cannot be measured in money, but wealth that is measured in love, education, care, and a sense of security.

This community has produced such people as Nikki Giovanni, a great poet and educator; Dr. Charles Green, president of Bermuda College in the Bermudas; Dr. Patricia Randolph Leigh, author of *Fly in the Ointment*; the late Dr. Charles Folds, singer, songwriter, and Grammy Award winner; songwriter Charles Spurling; the Isley Brothers; Clyde Brown, noted musician; Carl Westmoreland, a noted historian working at the National Underground Railroad Freedom Center; and Rev. Damon Lynch, who is on the board of the National Underground Freedom Center; actor Hari Rhodes; actor Clarence Williams; the late Mae Faggs Starr, Olympic gold medalist in track at the 1952 Helsinki games; William DeHart Hubbard, Olympic star in the 1924 Paris games for the running board jump and manager of the Valley Homes Mutual Housing; and Leslie Edwards, a member of the Tuskegee Airmen. Other important people who come from Lincoln Heights include Dr. Fred Bronson and Dr. William Bronson; Dr. Annett Hardy; Dr. Gloria Walker; Dr. Stuart Harris, Dr. Marva Daniels Lawson; Dr. Ronald Murph, a dentist; the Hodge family, third-generation stonemasons, who picked and laid the stones for the National Underground Railroad Freedom Center; Charles Whitehead, former vice president of Ashland Oil in Ashland, Kentucky; and Alvin McCrudy, plant manager of the Miller Brewing Company in Trenton, Ohio. Lincoln Heights was also the home to the Rite Recording Company, where James Brown and other artists recorded their songs. Lincoln Heights is a community of rich black heritage and history.

One

IN THE BEGINNING

In the beginning, the residential area later named Lincoln Heights was composed of seven all-black subdivisions or communities: the Cincinnati Industrial Subdivision, the Cincinnati Industrial Subdivision Annex, Valley View, the Washington Subdivision, the Oak Park Subdivision, the Grandview Heights, and the Lincoln Heights Subdivision Annex. Several attempts were made to unite the Black Mill Creek Valley subdivisions. Leaders of the movement were James M. Hunter, Rev. Michael J. Mangham, Charles Anderson, William Phillips, Robert Flowers, and Jessie Daniels. The first obstacle was the naming of the community. Only three names were considered: Marianna, after local philanthropist Marianna Matthews; Lincoln Heights, after the country's 16th president; and Grandview Heights, the largest of the subdivisions.

The first petition to incorporate Lincoln Heights was filed on September 11, 1940, by Eugene Fulton, a young, black Cincinnati lawyer. Five weeks later, three local residents, Helen Collins, Thaddeus Harvey, and Major Zeigler, filed an injunction. Wright Aeronautical Corporation and Defense Plant Corporation plant manager W. W. Finlay testified against the incorporation of Lincoln Heights, stating plant officials had title to the entire Valley View subdivision, which was platted within the limits; the village's current boundaries made it unreasonably large; and Valley View involved no residential buildings.

A third petition was filed on February 22, 1944, without Valley View. On April 5, 1944, the commissioners opened the hearing, which ended with an indefinite postponement. However, the strong determination of the citizens of Lincoln Heights to be self-governing made the commissioners reconsider, and on June 14, 1944, the petition was granted. The county recorder was ordered to hold the petition for 60 days. On the 58th day, an injunction was filed against the incorporation. The petition for incorporation of Lincoln Heights stayed in the Hamilton county courts for five years. The next proceeding on August 22, 1945, was successful, with the Hamilton County Board of Commissioners passing a favorable verdict. Lincoln Heights became the first all-black, self-governing city north of the Mason-Dixon Line.

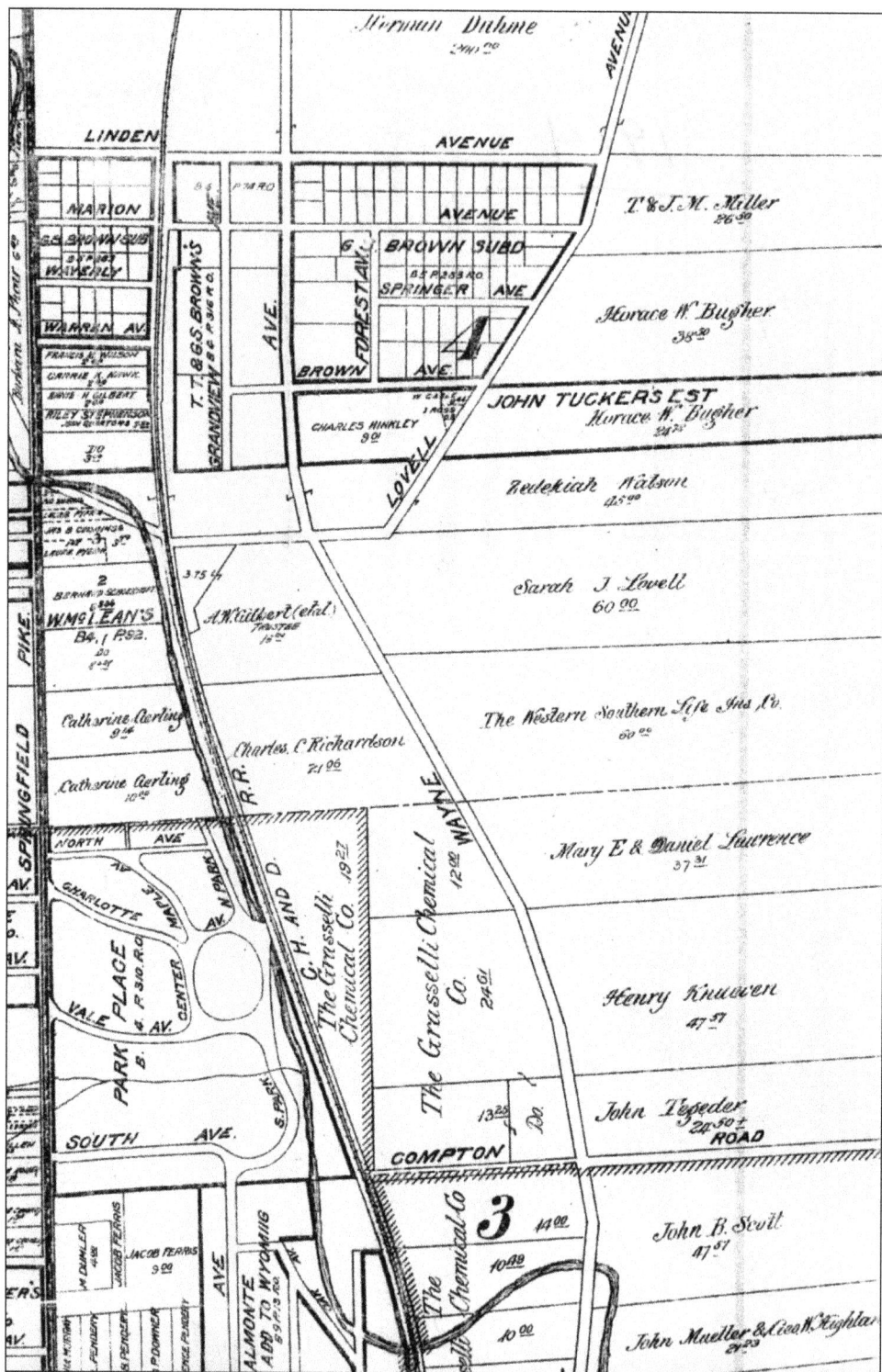

The 1914 Hamilton County atlas shows plats of townships, incorporated towns, and villages and maps of Greater Cincinnati. (Courtesy of the Public Library Cincinnati and Hamilton County.)

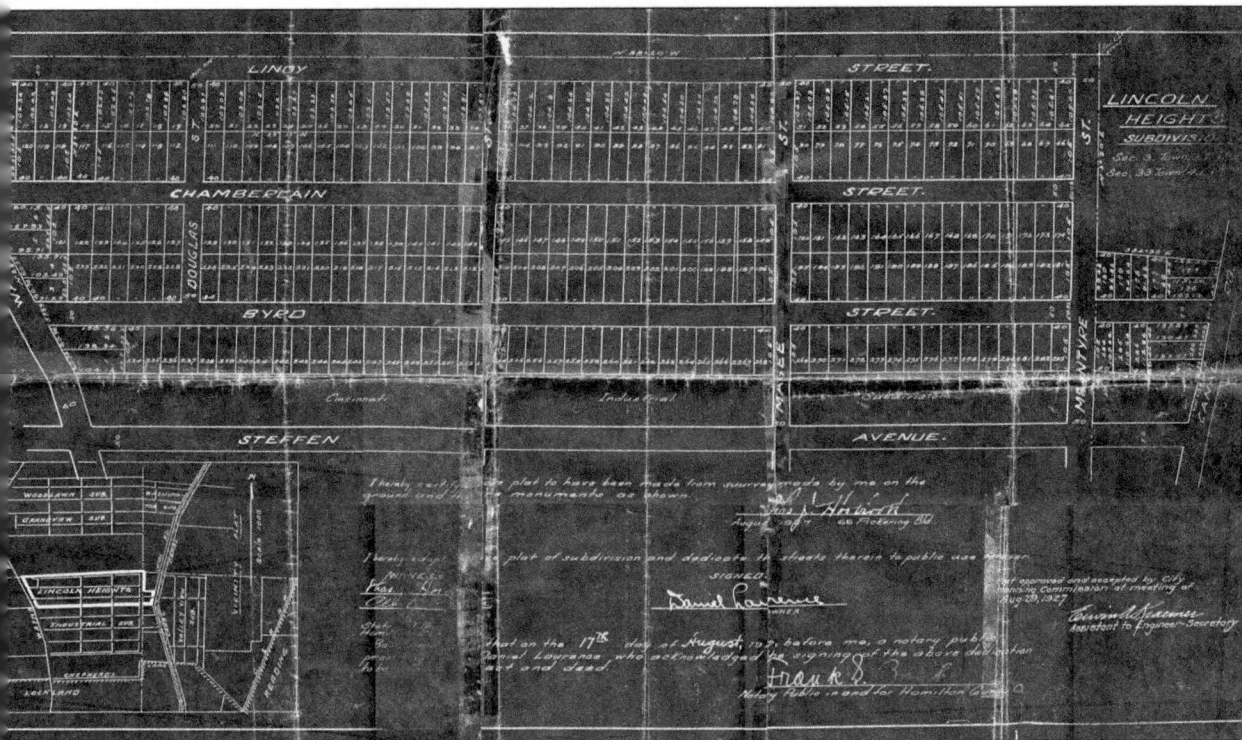

This is a platted map of the Lincoln Heights Subdivision dated August 29, 1927, signed by Charles J. Hosbrook. (Courtesy of the University of Cincinnati Archives and Rare Books.)

Mill Creek Valley

Woodlawn

Evendale

Lincoln Heights

4.

-37-

N

E   W

S

3.

1.

2.

1. Cincinnati Indus-
   trial Subdivision
2. Cincinnati Indus-
   trial Annex Sub-
   division
3. Valley View Sub-
   division
4. Washington Sub-
   division

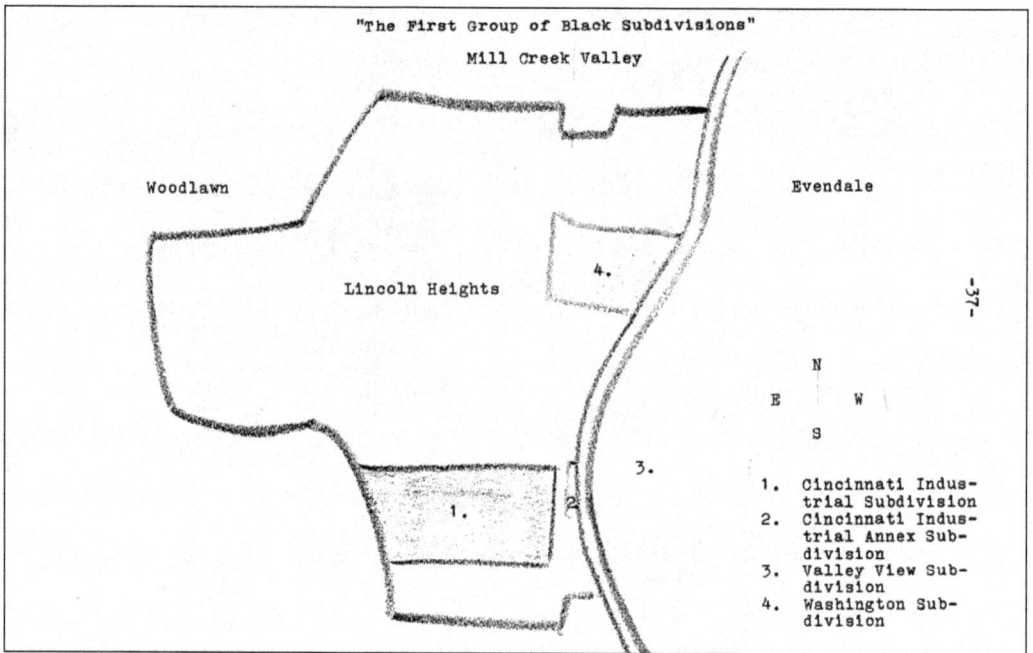

Pictured here is the first group of subdivisions of the Mill Creek Valley, consisting of Cincinnati Industrial Subdivision, Cincinnati Industrial Subdivision Annex, Valley View, and the Washington Subdivision, known as the lower subdivision of Lincoln Heights. (Courtesy of the University of Cincinnati.)

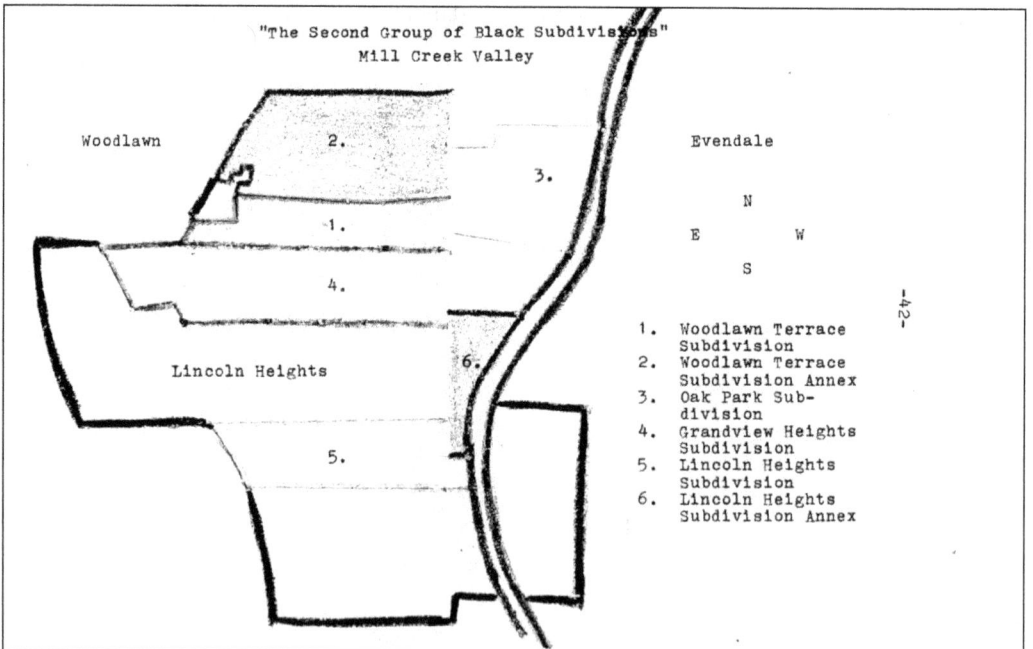

"The Second Group of Black Subdivisions"

Mill Creek Valley

Woodlawn

Evendale

2.

3.

N

E   W

S

-1.

4.

-42-

Lincoln Heights

6.

5.

1. Woodlawn Terrace
   Subdivision
2. Woodlawn Terrace
   Subdivision Annex
3. Oak Park Sub-
   division
4. Grandview Heights
   Subdivision
5. Lincoln Heights
   Subdivision
6. Lincoln Heights
   Subdivision Annex

This second group of subdivisions of the Mill Creek Valley consisted of Woodlawn Terrace Subdivision, Woodlawn Terrace Subdivision Annex, Oak Park Subdivision, Grandview Heights, Lincoln Heights Subdivision, and Lincoln Heights Subdivision Annex. (Courtesy of the University of Cincinnati.)

This is the original article dated March 1, 1941, from the *Cincinnati Enquirer* on Lincoln Heights filing incorporation papers to form New Negro Village near Wright Engine Plant. (Courtesy of Jeanette Crawford.)

Lincoln Heights Incorporation Is Held Invalid

Court Orders Cancellation of All Proceedings. 1941

Declaring invalid all proceedings in the incorporation of the all-Negro village of Lincoln Heights authorized at an election held months ago, Judge Alfred Mack in Common Pleas Court Monday ordered County Recorder George E. Kearns to cancel all record of the proceedings.

The decision was given in the suit of Mrs. Helen Collins, 18 Rose Street, Lockland postoffice, who filed suit through Attorneys William Thorndye and Ralph Becker to attack legality of the incorporation. Among the bases for the attack, Thorndyke and Becker argued that County Commissioners had exclusive jurisdiction in such matters and that therefore proceedings taken by Springfield Township trustees were invalid.

Upholding Thorndye and Becker's contention, Judge Mack pointed out that there was conflict in two Appellate Court decisions on that point, the Appellate Court of this district having held that the County Commissioners had exclusive jurisdiction while another court in Cuyahoga County held to the contrary. Judge Mack wrote that because of this conflict in the upper court decisions, the case undoubtedly would be certified to the Supreme Court.

RECALLS ELECTION

At last Tuesday's election the Rev. M. J. Mangham, Negro, pastor of the Woodlawn Baptist Church, was chosen to be the village's first mayor effective Jan. 1. All voting was by the "write-in" method, as there were no previously selected candidates. The Rev. Mangham received 303 votes. Other village officials also were elected at the same time.

Lincoln Heights Citizens File Incorporation Appeal

Residents of Lincoln Heights, Negro community north of Lockland, this week filed an appeal with the District Court in the matter of the incorporation of their community as a village. Recently the Court of Common Pleas of Hamilton County, by an opinion rendered by Judge Alfred Mack, held that incorporation proceedings approved by the Trustees of Springfield Township were invalid for the reason that only the County Commissioners have authority under the law to act in such matters. The appeal asks that the decision of the Common Pleas Court be set aside and that the incorporation be declared legal and valid.

For the reason that the findings of the Courts of Appeal in two counties are at variance relative to the question of authority to hear incorporation proceedings, it is likely that the matter will go at once to the Supreme Court of Ohio, that court never having handed down an opinion in the matter.

At the recent general election, residents of the community proceeded to elect village officials. Names of successful candidates were written in on the official ballot, no candidates having been nominated. It is likely that some weeks will pass before a decision can be had.

Here is the original newspaper article about Lincoln Heights's plans for incorporation of the community. (Courtesy of Jeanette Crawford.)

13

Village of Lincoln Heights, Ohio

CHARTER

Robert Flowers Civic Center
1100 Lindy Ave.

Municipal Building
1201 Steffens Ave.

Community Facilities Building
1171 Adams St.

May 4, 1993

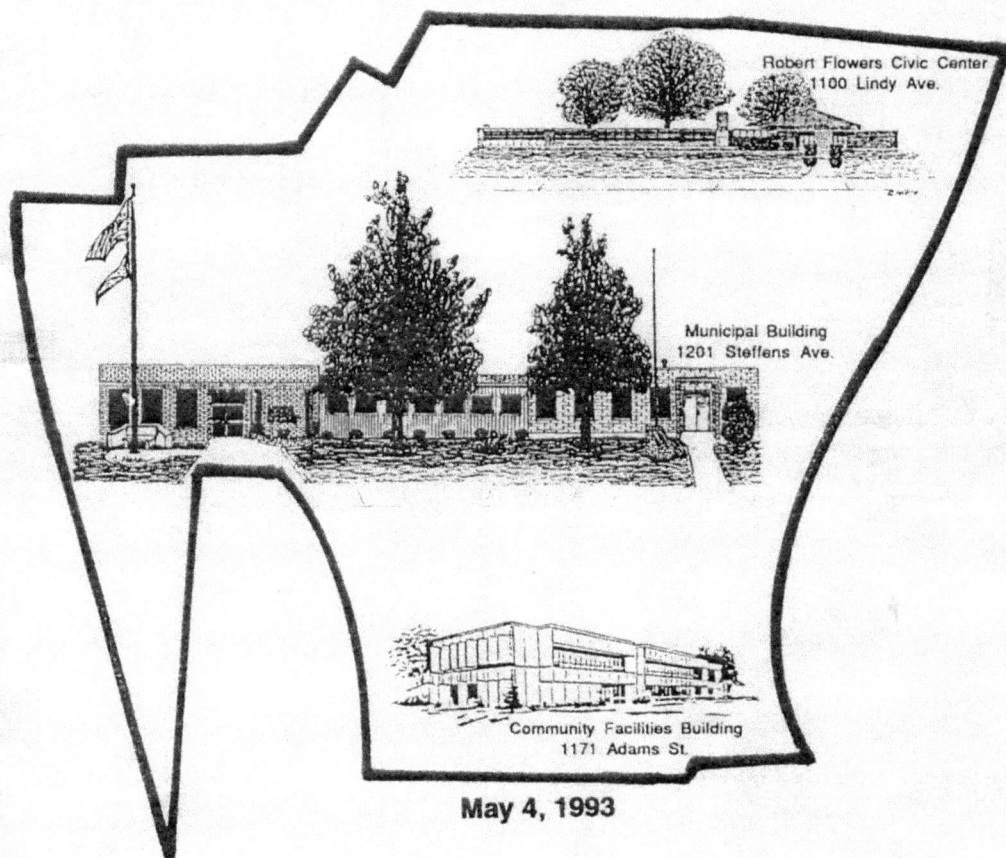

1974 Special Election: First Charter Adopted
1977: Charter Revised
1985: Charter Abolished
May, 1993 Primary Election: Charter Revised and Presented To Voters

Cover by:
Craig Hardy & Harold Stewart

Craig Hardy and Harold Stewart designed the charter cover of Lincoln Heights. The shape of this charter is that of the community of Lincoln Heights. (Author's collection.)

Pictured is Mike J. Mangham during the swearing-in ceremony for the first mayor for Lincoln Heights. Mangham was one of the foremost citizens in every civic enterprise in Lincoln Heights prior to incorporation. He worked with other citizens to secure water, sewers, fire equipment, and other improvements in the community. His perseverance as a proponent in the fight for incorporation of Lincoln Heights for nearly seven years is a testament of his great courage. (Courtesy of Mollie Mangham Spears.)

This is the first council for the Village of Lincoln Heights on January 1, 1947. From left to right are Rev. R. J. Wess, pastor of Lincoln Heights Missionary Baptist Church; Mayor Mike J. Mangham; Eugene Fulton, solicitor; Leroy Rice, councilman; Luke Craig, councilman; Luther T. Lyle, treasurer; Guy T. Westmoreland, village clerk; Arthur T. Shivers, councilman; Thomas Leigh Sr., councilman; James M. Hunter, councilman; Robert Flowers, councilman. (Courtesy of Mollie Mangham Spears.)

The community and ceremonial officials come together for the swearing-in ceremony of Mangham, the first mayor of Lincoln Heights, and the first council, including members Rice, Craig, Shivers, Leigh, Hunter, and Flowers in the old Lincoln Heights Elementary (formerly South Woodlawn) School. (Courtesy of Mollie Mangham Spears.)

From left to right, Harold Trice, Luther T. Lyle, Reverend Mangham, and Leroy J. Rice pose here at the Mount Moriah Baptist Church for special services of the day. (Courtesy of Mollie Mangham Spears.)

Gov. Thomas E. Dewey invited Mayor and Rev. Mike Mangham, Luke Craig, and other members of council to New York City for a ticker tape parade to honor Lincoln Heights as one of the few cities in America that were completely self-governing and African American. (Courtesy of Mollie Mangham Spears.)

Mayor Mangham is seen here in New York to greet members of the welcoming committee for Dewey. (Courtesy of Mollie Mangham Spears.)

Mayor Mangham is signing in at the hotel in New York City before the ticker tape parade. (Courtesy of Mollie Mangham Spears.)

Rev. Robert Flowers (left), service director, and Guy T. Westmoreland, auditor, are seen here sitting in Westmoreland's office on June 10, 1957. (Courtesy of Jeanette Crawford.)

From left to right, unidentified, Mayor Mike Mangham, Leroy Rice, and Police Chief Simm W. Thompson are pictured here in the village hall office of the mayor. (Courtesy of Mollie Mangham Spears.)

From left to right, James B. Rice, Oscar Grey, Ervin Martin, Sgt. Jewell Jett, Melvin Hayes, William Powell, and George Smith gather with Police Chief Thompson, sitting in a chair. Grey was the constable of Springfield Township. He was also a special deputy sheriff. (Courtesy of Mollie Mangham Spears.)

Chief Thompson (left) stands in front of the building along with, from left to right, an unidentified person, policeman Jett, and Guy T. Westmoreland of the village. (Courtesy of Mollie Mangham Spears.)

From left to right, Harry Howard Sr., Harry Howard Jr., and two unidentified officers stand in front of the police station. (Courtesy of Andrienne Howard.)

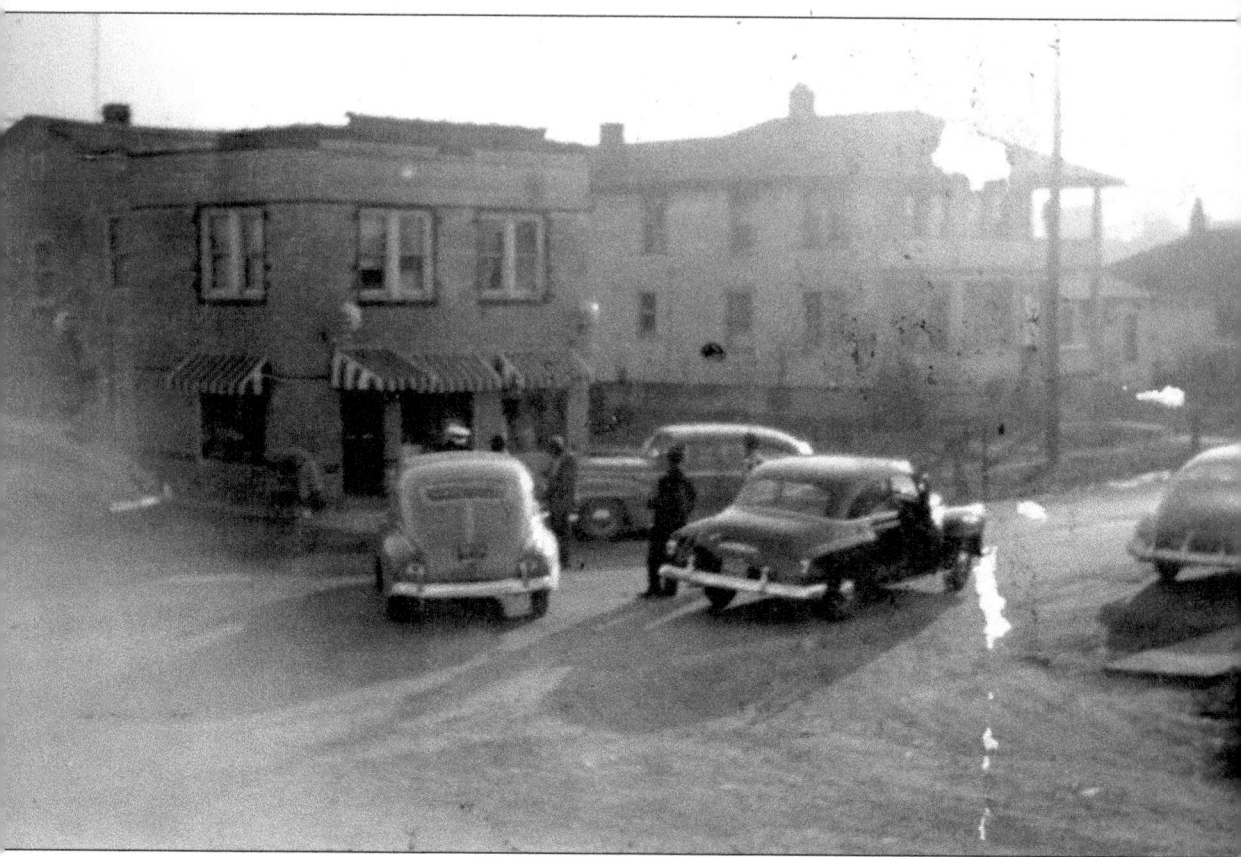

Lincoln Heights police officers make a stop at the corner of Van Buren and Douglas Streets. Simm W. Thompson was the first police chief. A county deputy whom Thompson knew asked him if he would like to become a special deputy in Hamilton County with primary emphasis on working in the subdivision, considering he had military police experience. Sheriff George Lutz appointed him in June 1935. (Courtesy of Columbus Cook.)

Lincoln Heights Volunteer Fire Department existed as the only African American volunteer group in the state of Ohio from a self-governing community. A small group of local residents met in 1933 to form a volunteer fireman's association under the leadership of Joe Bingham. The group purchased a little Hudson fire truck from the village of Lockland for approximately $800. Training was from the Cincinnati Fire Department. They put their lives on the line in the early days of Lincoln Heights's existence for the safety of the community. The fire truck stayed on Simmons Street with Deacon Don Ellis. From left to right are (first row) Chief Henry Lawson, Deacon Ellis, Rufus Mangham, and Ervin Martin; (second row) Love Flowers, Atward Neal, June Hunter, Theodore "Slim" Brown, Willie Lightener, Cecil Hunter, Ralph Jenkins, and James Rozier. (Courtesy of Winfred Mangham.)

Henry Lawson was determined to improve the quality of fire protection in the community. He called a meeting of several friends, including Cecil and June Hunter, Odell Boggs, George Lewis, Bog Brown, and several others. From left to right are (first row) Rufus Mangham, Love Flowers, Alvoteas Brown, Ralph Jenkins, and Henry Lawson; (second row) Calvin Tarver, Odell Boggs, unidentified, Jimmy Blessed, and Willie Lightner. (Courtesy of Winfred Mangham.)

Members of the Lincoln Heights Fire Department stand in front of the fire station in the village. From left to right are Walter Smith, Jenkins, Calvin Tarver, Willie Lindsay, Linzy Sanders, and Henry Lawson. (Courtesy of Mildred Lindsay Williams.)

24

The Lincoln Heights Volunteer Fire Department on engine No. 2, from left to right, are (first row) Cecil Hunter, William Clark, and Leonard Lawson; (second row) unidentified, Melvin Satterwhite, unidentified, and Elbert Daniels. (Courtesy of Mildred Lindsay Williams.)

Firemen on the trucks are getting ready to be in the Lincoln Heights Day Festival parade. Every year, the fire department drives the fire trucks for the parade. (Courtesy of Andrienne Howard.)

The Lincoln Heights Fire Department pose in front of the station in 1970. Laura McDay is wearing a banner as advertisement for a member of Congress. From left to right are William Clark, unidentified, Nennie Sanders, Mr. Hamilton, unidentified, Melvin Satterwhite, Charles Epps, Laura McDay, Allan Matthews, Wilbert Lewis, Cecil Hunter, and Alvoteas Brown; (on truck) Thomas Moxley, William D. Boggs, and Marshall Hardy. (Courtesy of Mollie Mangham Spears.)

Unidentified residents visit the fire department on the day of the Lincoln Heights Day Festival parade. (Courtesy of Andrienne Howard.)

Two

HEARING GOD'S WORDS

There are several churches in Lincoln Heights, including Lincoln Heights Missionary Baptist, Ebenezer Second Baptist, New Friendship Baptist, Revealed Holiness Church of God, St. Martin DePorres, St. Simon of Cyrene Episcopal Church, Tabernacle, and others. But Lincoln Heights Missionary Baptist, Tabernacle, and Ebenezer Second Baptist were started from Mount Moriah Baptist Church, the mother church of the community. The idea for Mount Moriah Baptist's place of worship was conceived in 1925 by Rev. Joseph Hudson, a Cincinnati evangelist, and William Rozier, a resident of the "sub." Through their leadership, the first service was held under a bush harbor. As winter approached, the Haley-Livingston Land Company noticed the need of the group and offered to sell lot 159 to the church trustees on April 16, 1925. Hudson was the first pastor and Rozier, George W. Belt, Willie Byrd, Henry Brown, George Lewis, and Henry-Moseley were the trustees.

Mount Moriah Baptist Church deacons and trustees of 1930 are seen here. From left to right are (first row) unidentified, unidentified, Rev. Charles Wesley, and Rev. Albert Armstrong,; (second row) Rev. Earl Wagner, Deacon William Rozier, unidentified, and unidentified; (third row) Deacon Clark, Deacon Joseph Pickens, and Deacon Rufus Fears. Rozier bought the first load of used lumber to build a temporary place of worship, a shedlike building, which was torn down when this church was built. (Courtesy of Angie Foster Thompson.)

Wesley the fourth pastor of the church and the congregation in front of Mount Moriah Baptist Church on Simmons Street in 1930s. Mount Moriah was the first church in the newly created subdivision. (Courtesy of Angela Foster Thompson.)

Wesley and members of the church are pictured at a conference at Mount Moriah Baptist Church on Simmons Street. Identified here are Wesley, Ruby Hillman, Walter Hillman, Ed Smith, Rev. Lucas Daniels, Deacon Howard Wilkerson, and Deacon James Stweard. (Courtesy of Angela Foster Thompson.)

The board of trustees for Mount Moriah Baptist Church are seen here. Identified are James Wilkerson, Homer Greenwood, Dickey Powell, Frank Perry, Deacon James Stewart, Rev. Samuel Stewart, George Wilkerson, James Vinegar, Burt Harris, John Wars, Walter Hillman, Paul Jenkins, Deacon Rufus Fears, Deacon Raymond Green, J. L. Wilkerson, Ted Hall, and Willie James Roberts. James Stewart was chairman of this group, and Frank Perry Jr. was chairman of the board of trustees. (Courtesy of Angela Foster Thompson.)

LOIS PERRY

Lois Perry is dressed for an old-timers costume day at the Mount Moriah Baptist Church. Perry was one of the pioneering family members of Lincoln Heights, moving there in the early 1930s. (Courtesy of Angela Foster Thompson.)

Here are young adult ushers at Mount Moriah Baptist Church. From left to right are (first row) unidentified, Angela Foster, Venora Summeour, Annie Wimberly, Carolyn Davis, Georgia Wimberly, Miram Lynch, and Tommy Baker; (second row) Ann Jones, Rose Carr, Anna Perry, Jett Lynch, Sandra Davis, Carol Elliott, Shelia Turner, Donna Wilkerson, Benelia Wilkinson, Hazel Wimberly, and Deidre Robinson; (third row) Helen Jefferson, Lester Tooson, Ulysses Brown, Shelia Harris, Ronnie Martin, and Randall Hamilton. (Courtesy of Angela Foster Thompson.)

Mount Moriah Baptist Church ushers were servants for the Lord each and every Sunday. (Courtesy of Angela Foster Thompson.)

Mount Moriah Baptist Church men and women ushers were ready to serve the congregation each week. (Courtesy of Angela Foster Thompson.)

Mount Moriah Baptist Church Children's Choir sang with the voices of angels. The children were always ready to sing. Standing is Ruby Hillman (left). (Courtesy of Angela Foster Thompson.)

Pictured here is the Mount Moriah Baptist Church Adult Choir. Pastor Charles Wesley is standing with Sally Isley (mother of the Isley Brothers) who was the pianist and director of the senior choir. She also taught beginner and advance piano lessons. (Courtesy of Angela Foster Thompson.)

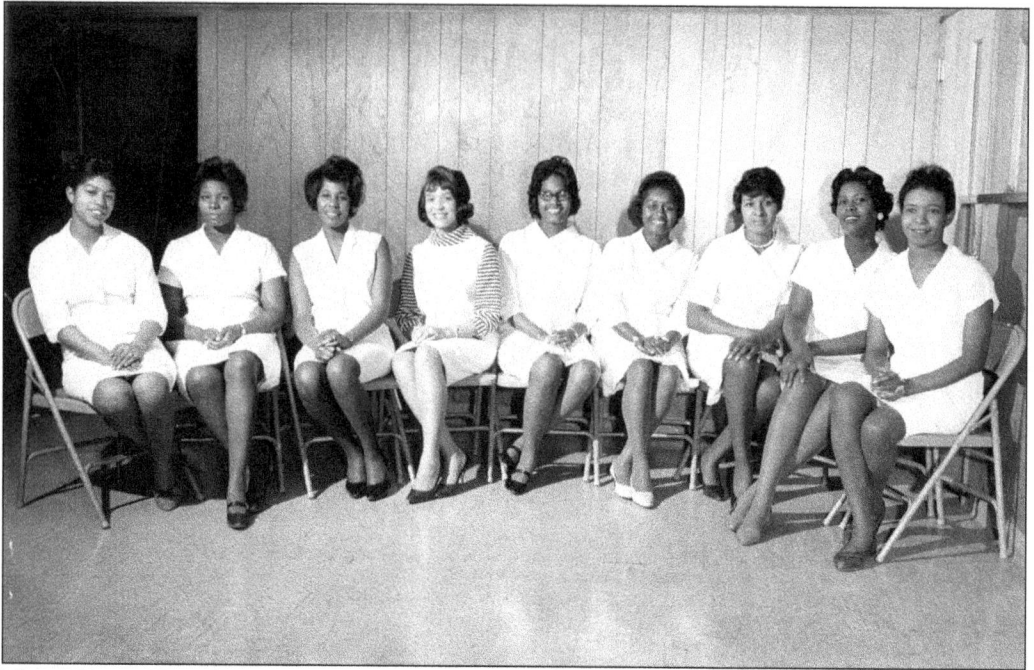

The Mount Moriah Young Matrons pose here. From left to right are Donna Wilkerson, unidentified, unidentified, Ann Jones, Patricia McDowell, Quincy Davis, Betty Robinson, Venetta Lynch, and Allis King Young. (Courtesy of Angela Foster Thompson.)

The 1940 senior choir of Mount Moriah Baptist Church poses here. Sitting second from the left is the author's grandmother Lois Perry, and far to the right is Rev. Charles Wesley. (Courtesy of Patricia McDowell.)

34

This is the senior choir of Lincoln Heights Missionary Baptist Church. From left to right are (first row) unidentified, Mildred Lindsay, Rev. Richard D. Wess, Beulah Wess, unidentified, and Lula Level; (second row) Willie Lindsay, Ruth Gray, Marian McClure, unidentified, Charles Folds, Patsy Williams, unidentified, Mrs. Lumas, and unidentified. The Lincoln Heights Missionary Baptist Church choir director was Mrs. Jefferies. Jefferies always made the choir dress differently. Lincoln Heights Missionary Baptist Church was formed on August 26, 1928, when a group of 28 disciples for Christ split from Mount Moriah Baptist Church over personality differences. (Courtesy of Mildred Lindsay Williams.)

The Lincoln Heights Missionary Baptist Church male chorus poses here. From left to right are (first row) Rev. Prentiss Brown Sr., Willie Lindsay, unidentified, and unidentified; (second row) Deacon James Gray, unidentified, Willie Farrow, and Wilbert Dowdy; (third row) James McCoy, Rev. Clarence Carruth, Freddie Folds, and Deacon James Lowery; (fourth row) Deacon Andy Jones, and Bob Barber. (Courtesy of Mildred Lindsay Williams.)

The Lincoln Heights Missionary Baptist Church holds their senior recital with Rev. Richard D. Wess and Beulah Wess. From left to right are (first row) T. J. Malone, unidentified, Beulah Wess, and Reverend Wess; (second row) Lula Level, Cassie Morris, Mrs. Robert Downs, Bert Snow, Mrs. Shepherd, unidentified, Katherine Brooks, and Marian McClure; (third row) Margaret Allen, Donna Thomas, Prentiss Brown, Willie Lindsay, Wilbert Dowdy, unidentified, Mrs. McCoy, Deacon James Gray, unidentified, Mildred Lindsay, and Myrtis Davis. (Courtesy of Mildred Lindsay Williams.)

The Lincoln Heights Missionary Baptist Church and the female ushers are seen here with Rev. R. D. Wess in the middle of the row. God's servants are in the church. (Courtesy of Mildred Williams Lindsay.)

The Lincoln Heights Missionary Baptist Church senior choir is pictured here. Identified here are Hazel Shumper, Marian McClure, Mrs. Robert Down, Katherine Brooks, Reverend Wess, Mrs. Wess, Mrs. Higgins, Donna Thomas MacFee, Cassie Morris, Elouise ?, Mrs. Love, Mrs. McCoy, Mrs. Lumas, Mrs. Simmons, Margaret Allen, Elizabeth Price, Lattie Holland, Myrtis Davis, Mrs. Shepherd's daughter, Mrs. Lowry, Mr. Higgins, Mr. McCoy, Mr. Lindsey, Decon Wilbert Dowdy, Charles Fold, and Barbara Hall. (Courtesy of Mildred Williams Lindsay.)

Three

ST. SIMON OF CYRENE

St. Simon of Cyrene Episcopal Church was the first parish building in Lincoln Heights. In 1879, a baby girl was born in Glendale and was given the name of Eva Lee Matthews. In her adult life, she became Mother Eva Mary, founder of the Episcopal Sisterhood of the Transfiguration and of Bethany Home for girls—both started in 1898. The second mother of the community, chosen to succeed Mother Eva Mary, was Sr. Beatrice Martha. In the fall of 1930, Sr. Beatrice Martha told Sr. Olivia Mary to think about a growing black community on the hill that would need a church, a great missionary opportunity. The house on the corner of Independence and Douglas Streets had not only been purchased but also renovated and furnished. Through the throwing together of two rooms, a chapel was made ready for an opening service on the evening of February 9, 1931. The sister's chaplain, Father Lewis, held that service and thereafter officiated there every Sunday, while the sisters organized a Sunday school and a sewing school held on Saturdays. The property included two lots in addition to the one where the house stood. The present rectory stood on the western-most lot, which has a garage on the property. The Reverend Arthur G. Wilson, who was at the time without a parish, became the full-time priest with the help of Mother Beatrice Martha.

St. Simon of Cyrene Episcopal Church was used as the rectory and the clinic for the community. During the Depression, Rev. Arthur G. Wilson helped those in the community by making sure the community needs were taken care of. (Courtesy of Rose Holloway.)

This is the first vacation church school for St. Simon of Cyrene in the early 1930s. The theme was God's will. (Courtesy of Rose Holloway.)

St. Simon of Cyrene is pictured here in the early days, along with one of the sisters and the children. (Courtesy of Rose Holloway.)

The first junior department in 1931 included Essie Williams and Evie Taylor as the assistant, who pose here. (Courtesy of Rose Holloway.)

Here is Fr. Raleigh Hariston and nuns for St. Simon of Cyrene. (Courtesy of Rose Holloway.)

One of the early vacation Bible school classes for St. Simon of Cyrene is pictured here along with staff members. (Courtesy of Rose Holloway.)

The fashion show committee gathers together to prepare for the upcoming event. It is one of the highlights for the year. (Courtesy of Rose Holloway.)

This group of members of St. Simon of Cyrene sits and enjoys fellowship with each other. This loyal group was dedicated to attending services every week. From left to right are Bernice Fields, M. Peeks, S. Hunter, and M. Price. Fields had the first marriage in the church. (Courtesy of Rose Holloway.)

Seen here is the vacation Bible school of 1933. It is one of the earliest classes of children at St. Simon School. (Courtesy of Rose Holloway.)

The Young Church Men's Group is seen in this photograph, with women attending. (Courtesy of Rose Holloway.)

The Young People's Center is where children went to play pool, read books, and have fun. From left to right are unidentified, Herbert Baxter, Louise Arlen Williams, Arthur Green, and Lewis Welles. (Courtesy of Rose Holloway.)

St. Simon School, pictured here in 1931, was opened as the result of the daily vacation Bible school in the summer. Parents asked the sisters to open a school because the children had a long way to walk over the muddy roads. The nearest school was on the corner of Steffens Street. (Courtesy of Rose Holloway.)

The St. Simon School class of 1937–1938 is pictured here with children sitting on the porch of the school. (Courtesy of Rose Holloway.)

Children seen here are getting their lessons and are under the careful watch of the nuns. (Courtesy of Rose Holloway.)

Staff members of St. Simon of Cyrene pose for the camera. (Courtesy of Rose Holloway.)

This sister from the Sisters of the Transfiguration shows her students the words of the day. (Courtesy of Rose Holloway.)

This is the first eighth grade graduating class of St. Simon School. (Courtesy of Rose Holloway.)

One of the first members of St. Simon of Cyrene, Alfred Redd, joined in early 1931. (Courtesy of Rose Holloway.)

The classroom says the Pledge of Allegiance before the day's work is to begin. (Courtesy of Rose Holloway.)

Harvey Redd, another member who joined St. Simon of Cyrene in 1931, was a Boy Scout leader for over 22 years. (Courtesy of Rose Holloway.)

Children in their smocks enjoy the art of painting in their kindergarten class at St. Simon School. (Courtesy of Rose Holloway.)

Sr. Virginia Cecelia's classroom is seen here. (Courtesy of Rose Holloway.)

Sister Josephine takes the children outside for an art lesson. (Courtesy of Rose Holloway.)

Eva Redd sits in conversation with the priest. She joined St. Simon of Cyrene in 1931. She was president of the Episcopal Church Women (ECW) and a member of the Chessaur Club. (Courtesy of Rose Holloway.)

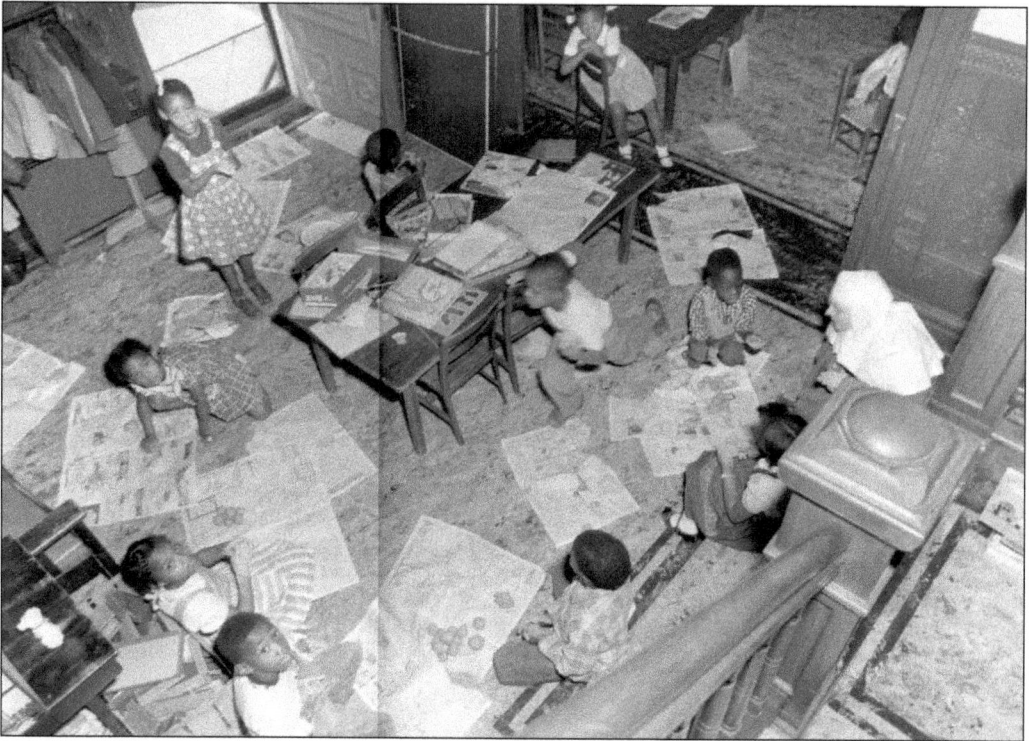
Sr. Winifred Agnes's classroom is pictured here at St. Simon School. (Courtesy of Rose Holloway.)

Fr. John Burgess and other members of the St. Simon Group work diligently in the church. From left to right are (first row) Sister Esther Mary, KeKe Williams, Essie Williams, and Father Burgess; (second row) James Mobley, Ivan Reynolds, Kenneth Graham, Carl Westmoreland, and Merven Stenston. (Courtesy of Rose Holloway.)

Fr. Peter Golden and Fr. John Burgess are seen here. (Courtesy of Rose Holloway.)

Mother Superior Olivia was the founder of the Episcopal Sisterhood of the Transfiguration and Bethany Home for girls in 1898. (Courtesy of Rose Holloway.)

Intermediate boys pose here with Miss Wilcox (left) and Sr. Ester Mary (right). Pictured are George Hughes, Chester Anderson, George Jones, Franklin Shands, Eugene Jetter, "Buster" Reynolds, Elmer Lewis, Ernest Myrick, Edward Shands, Willis Hitchcock, Arthur Williams, James Neal, John Jader, Carl Thomas, Eugene Easley, Taylor Hughs, Glover Evans, Edgar Shands, Jimmie Lee Shands, and George Humm. (Courtesy of Rose Holloway.)

Bishop Herbert Thompson, one of the faithful for St. Simon of Cyrene, serves the community to hear the word of God. (Courtesy of Rose Holloway.)

Four

BUILT BY THE PEOPLE FOR THE PEOPLE

The land transactions in Woodlawn Terrace were interesting. Most of these dealings involved Willis Harper of the Harper Realty Company and James H. Cleveland, a local attorney, both of whom served as agents for Marianna Matthews, the widow of the renowned lawyer Mortimer Matthews. Marianna Matthews was the daughter of William A. and Elizabeth Procter of Procter and Gamble Soap Company. Her husband, Mortimer, was a highly successful businessman and lawyer, whose practice dealt with corporation and real estate law.

Marianna Matthews was a philanthropist who saw in the upper Mill Creek Valley settlement an opportunity to contribute to the resolution of the housing problem. She was influenced by Joseph Schmidlapp and believed that it was possible to profitably construct low-rent housing for the poor. Harper and Cleveland purchased all of the lots in the Woodlawn Terrace for Marianna Matthews. In the early 1930s, Cleveland purchased 10 lots from Albert Armstrong, and on December 9, 1936, he acquired seven lots from the Harper Realty Company. By December 1942, Cleveland purchased all of the lots owned by both Harper and Armstrong. The majority of these lots were located in the extreme western portion of Woodlawn Terrace. On February 15, 1943, the lots were transferred to Marianna Matthews and then to the Norris Homes, of which she was president.

Norris Homes was founded to build and sell houses as a land-house unit to blacks who lived in the Mill Creek Valley. Marianna Matthews's son Stanley, who was an architect, designed the housing project. The Wallendon Corporation, a local firm, financed all the homes for over a 25-year period at a cost of $27.52 per month. To provide for spiritual and moral development of those who lived in the housing project, the Matthews' arranged for the Sisters of the Transfiguration from Glendale to purchase five lots adjacent to the Norris Homes project. Mortimer Matthews had been a trustee and vice president of the Sisters of the Transfiguration, and two of their daughters, Olivia and Catherine, were sisters in the Convent of Transfiguration.

Seen here is the Valley Homes Mutual Housing Cooperation community building along with the barracks. Property for this project was purchased from Frank and Rose Medosch who had a farm on the land. The project was originally called Valley View Homes and was built in 1941 as a 350-unit housing project for defense workers at the Wright Aeronautical Plant (now General Electric). It was an all-black project. Valley Homes was managed for the U.S. Public Housing Administration by the Cincinnati Metropolitan Housing Authority (CMHA). Franklin D. Roosevelt, president of the CMHA Federal Works Agency, said "These homes were built by the people of the United States for the defenders of this nation." (Courtesy of Adrienne Howard.)

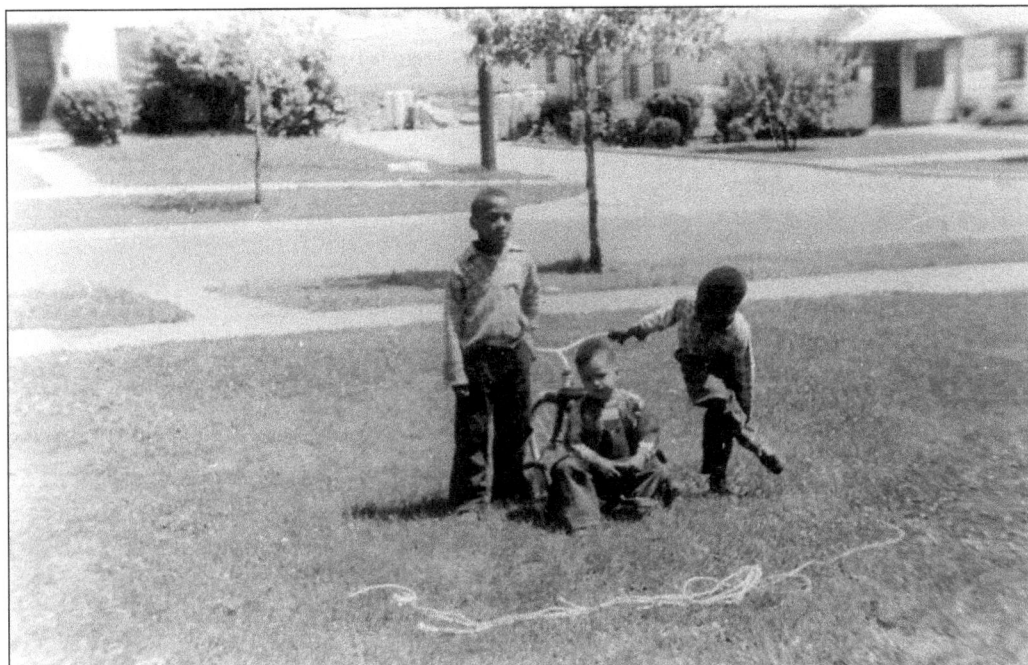

Harry Howard Jr. (center) and friends play in the yard on Medosch Street across from the Valley Homes office. In the background is the one-level structure called the barracks. (Courtesy of Adrienne Howard.)

From left to right, Deborah, Harry, and Theadora Howard are pictured here in the parking lot of the Valley Homes on a Sunday afternoon. (Courtesy of Adrienne Howard.)

Harry and Adrienne Howard are in their front yard in the Valley Homes. (Courtesy of Adrienne Howard.)

Harry Howard (left) and Lonnie Bennett pose in their front yard on Medosch Street. This is the land that Frank and Rose Medosch sold. That is the reason the street is named in honor of the Medosch family. (Courtesy of Adrienne Howard.)

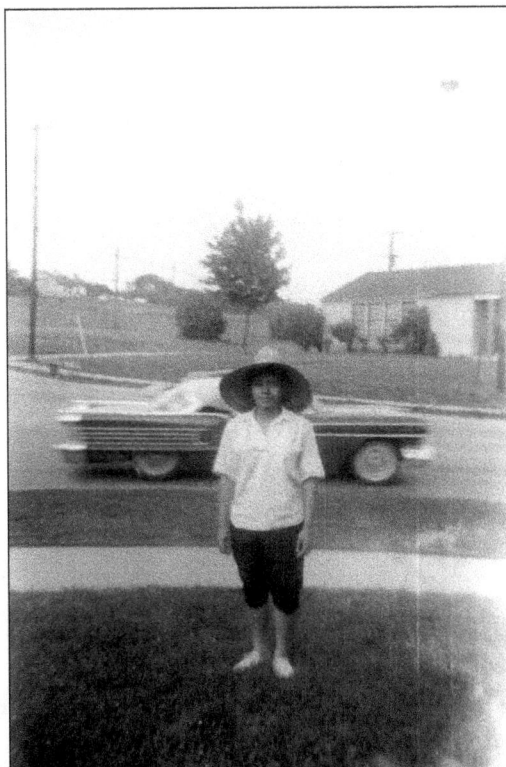

Emily Hunt, longtime resident of the village of Lincoln Heights, stands in her yard in the Valley Homes. (Courtesy Emily Hunt Stewart.)

Carolyn Davis stands in the parking lot on South Leggett in the Valley Homes. (Author's collection.)

Ladies in front of the Valley Homes community building dress in their Sunday best. From left to right are (first row) Carol Diggs and unidentified; (second row) unidentified, Genevieve Satterwhite, Ann Turner, Bernadette Love, and Barbara Gale Hendrix. (Courtesy of Marietta Roseman.)

Children stand in front of Oak Park Apartments (later changed to James W. Jones Apartments after pastor James Wesley Jones of Mount Moriah Baptist Church). The Dunn family supplied the land. (Courtesy of Angela Foster Thompson.)

Guy T. Westmoreland (left) and Deacon James Wilkerson show plans for the new Oak Park apartment complex. This 72-unit housing development was started on May 2, 1971. (Courtesy of Angela Foster Thompson.)

People of the community, members of Mount Moriah Baptist Church, and Rev. Damon Lynch II participate in the groundbreaking ceremony for the construction of Oak Park Apartments. These apartments were the brainchild of Rev. James W. Jones. (Courtesy of Angela Foster Thompson.)

Reverend Jones is seen here in the opening ceremony for the Oak Park Apartments along with members of the community and congregants of Mount Moriah Baptist Church. (Courtesy of Angela Foster Thompson.)

The Oak Park Apartments sign is seen here in front of the buildings. The name was later changed to the James W. Jones Apartments. (Courtesy of Angela Foster Thompson.)

The Oak Park Apartments were affordable living spaces for the residents in Lincoln Heights. They were a blessing in disguise, because it helped with the housing shortage in the community. (Courtesy of Angela Foster Thompson.)

Here some housing is being constructed in the early 1950s. Columbus Cook's mother's house is a blockhouse, which is made out of brick. (Courtesy of Columbus Cook.)

These old houses were built before Martin Luther King Estates were constructed. (Courtesy of Columbus Cook.)

One of the first houses built in Lincoln Heights was constructed by James Hunter. This is the home of Winfred Mangham. (Courtesy of Winfred Mangham.)

This is the Howards' house in Lincoln Heights on Steffens Street. Policeman Harry Howard Sr. lived here with his family very close to the village hall at the corner of Magee and Steffens Streets. Notice the gravel road and the way the mailboxes are out in front of the house. (Courtesy of Adrienne Howard.)

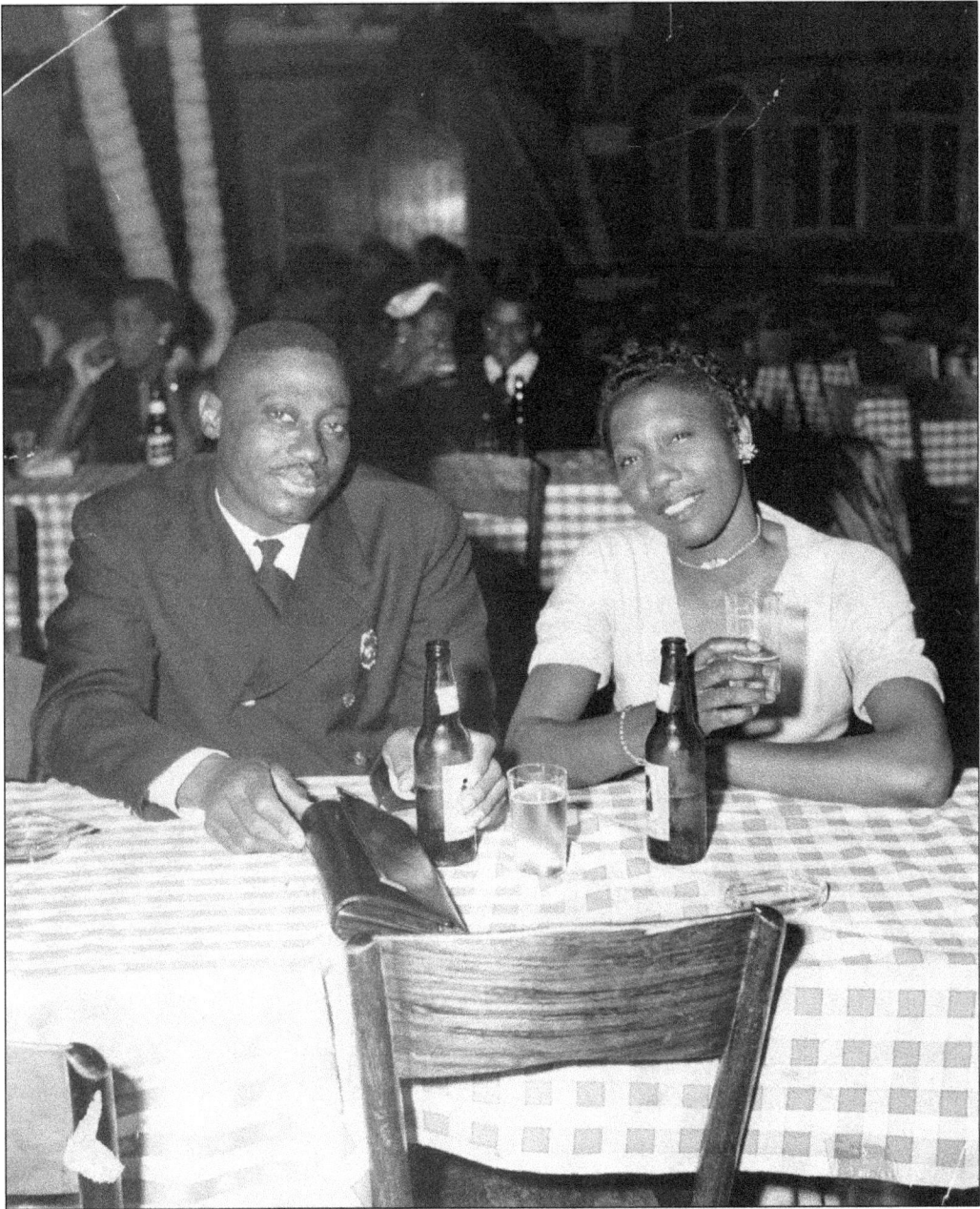

George Lewis and his wife, Susie McDade Lewis, are at Club Ebony. George Lewis was one of the most popular builders in Lincoln Heights. He built over 100 structures in the community. He was instrumental in building Club Ebony, Johnson Skating Rink, Mann's Lounge (which was named after Richard Lewis's son), Magic Moment, and several other structures. He also helped build Byrd Street Church (Lincoln Heights Missionary Baptist Church), Lincoln Heights Fire Station, and others. (Courtesy of Richard Lewis.)

Ralph Smith is one of the employees of George Lewis's construction company. Here Smith is working on a building in Hazelwood. Smith was an owner of the only slaughterhouse on Steffens Street in Lincoln Heights. (Courtesy of Richard Lewis.)

Several unidentified employees are working on the building being built by George Lewis's company in Hazelwood. (Courtesy of Richard Lewis.)

Frances Lewis is standing in front of Club Ebony, styling and profiling. The club was first called Lewis Lounge. It had every big band coming to the club that was traveling south. They stopped by the club to perform, including groups such as Lynn Hope, Tassel Zachery, and others. One night, George Lewis went to the club, and a combo was playing a song called "Ebony after Midnight." The next day, he changed the name of the club to Club Ebony. In the club on the north side was the dairy bar, in the middle of the club was an open ballroom, which was used for roller-skating, and on the south side was the cocktail lounge where big bands played. (Courtesy of Richard Lewis.)

ADVANCE TICKET

Paul Williams with Larry Darnell
and Acts
Lewis Roller Rink
Cor. Wayne and Simmons - Lincoln Heights
SATURDAY, MARCH 25 - 9:00 to 1:00

Advance Admission $1.25

For Reservations
Call PO 1266

This is an advance ticket to the Lewis Roller Rink inside Club Ebony, which cost $1.25 to get in. (Courtesy of Richard Lewis.)

Members of the community are enjoying themselves inside the Club Ebony. Clockwise from bottom left to right are Mr. Crockett, owner of the Crockett Drug Store; unidentified; George Lewis; Mrs. Lyons; Totem Lyons; Susie Lewis; unidentified; unidentified; Dr. Crockell, who delivered babies in Lincoln Heights; Luke Craig, a councilman; and Police Chief Simm W. Thompson. (Courtesy of Richard Lewis.)

Club Ebony and its distinguished guests are pictured here. From left to right are Mayor Reid of Lockland, George Lewis, Reverend Zellars, Mrs. Sherman, and Jesse Sherman. (Courtesy of Richard Lewis.)

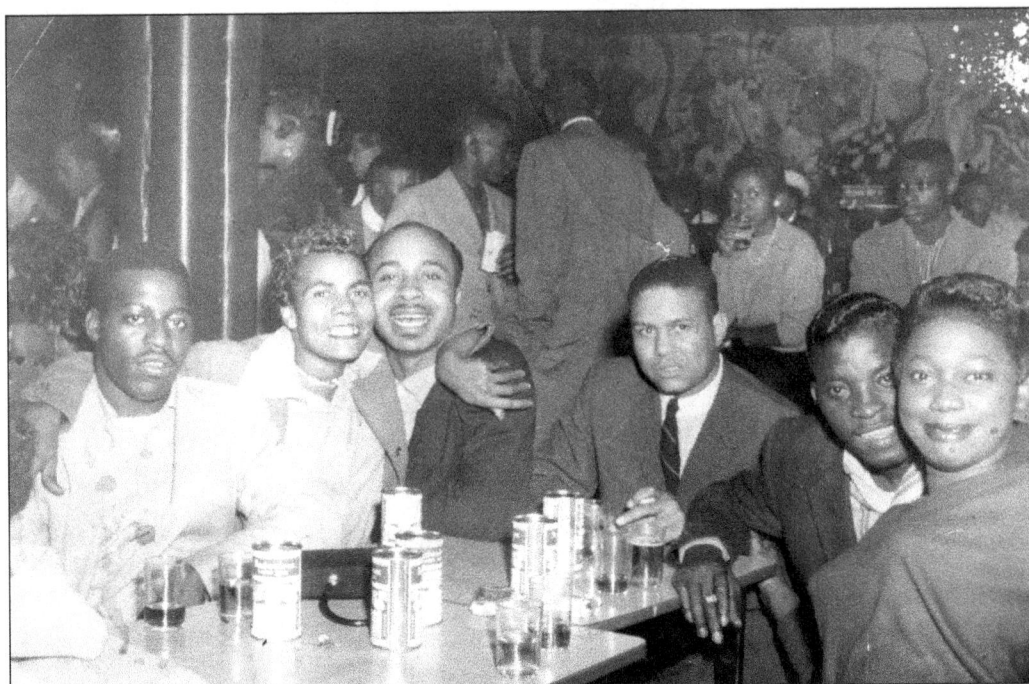

Even the members of the Perry family are enjoying a night out on the town at Club Ebony. From left to right are John "Bunchy" Perry, Virgilean Perry, Phil Perry, Theadore Boggs, Q. Whitt Mackey, and Jeanette Lewis. (Courtesy of Richard Lewis.)

George Lewis (left) enjoys the company of his friends at Club Ebony. (Courtesy of Richard Lewis.)

From left to right, George Lewis, Susie Lewis, Paul Jenkins, Eleanor Jenkins, unidentified, Jesse Sherman, unidentified, unidentified, and Georgiann Lewis are all enjoying the club. (Courtesy of Richard Lewis.)

Wiley's house in Lincoln Heights was built by George Lewis's construction company. He built the first split level in Lincoln Heights. (Courtesy of Richard Lewis.)

The community of Lincoln Heights did not have a regular bus service to provide for its residents like the city of Cincinnati did. Transportation for this community was done by an old bus someone drove from Lincoln Heights to the corner of Anthony Wayne and Wyoming Avenues in Lockland. (Courtesy of Adrienne Howard.)

The community center on Adams Street was where the Health Care Connection and sometimes community functions were held. Lincoln Heights Alumni Association often held the gathering of the Lincoln Heights High School's class reunions. (Courtesy of Deborah Seay.)

The community swimming pool of the village was where residents came together to help with a common goal of raising funds to build it. The pool was a popular attraction for the community for the first time in a long time. (Courtesy Deborah Seay.)

The Lincoln Heights Board of Directors recognizes the following people of the community: Cosa Blair, Carl J. Barkhardt (owner of Rite Records), Oliver H. Lackey Sr., Killis Moxley, and Guy T. Westmoreland. (Courtesy of Deborah Cameron.)

Honoree's For This Year's Awards

Rosa Blair, born in Evergreen, Alabama, moved to Lincoln Heights in December 1950, after graduating from Miles College with her A.B. Degree. Rosa and her husband Bruce H. Blair are the proud parents of Bruce H. Blair Jr., Robert J. Blair, Shirley J. Blair and Lyla Rose Blair. Ms. Blair has worked for the City of Lincoln Heights a total of twenty-three (23) years, in such positions as Clerk of Council, Auditor's Clerk, Finance Coordinator, and is presently Acting Finance Director. Present activities include: member of Towns Chapel, AME Church, Lincoln Heights Voters League, Bryant-Thompson Memorial Club, Lincoln Heights Democratic Club and Miles College Alumni Association, just to name a few.

Carl J. Barkhardt, owner of Rite Records was born in Cincinnati, Ohio on December 13, 1906. Mr. Burkhardt, opened his record manufacturing company in the city of Lincoln Heights in 1960, and has recently expanded his operation to be the largest record manufacturing plant in the entire midwest. Carl and his wife Lydia Burkhardt are the proud parents of Phillip Burkhardt and Sally Smith. The Burkhardts reside in the City of Wyoming.

Oliver H. Lackey Sr., veteran councilman, has been serving the City of Lincoln Heights as a council member for 23 consecutive years. Lackey lived in Cincinnati's West End as a child before his family moved to Lincoln Heights. Lackey's family was among the first to settle in Lincoln Heights in about 1929. Lackey, who survives his wife Betty Lackey, is the father of Carol Lackey, Ada Lackey and son, Oliver Lackey Jr.

Killis Moxley, born in LCincinnati, Ohio in 1918, is the owner of Moxley's Market. Moxley is a member of Saint Martin de Porres Church and is active with a member of Civil Organizations. Kellis and Eugenia Moxley, are the parents of Killis Moxley Jr., Michael Moxley and Renee Little.

Guy T. Westmoreland,Sr., former Auditor and Clerk of Council for the City of Lincoln Heights is presently serving as Field Representative for the Ohio Lottery Commission. Westmoreland, attended Chase College and Xavier University, where he majored in Business Administration. He has lived in the Valley Area since childhood and is married to Mildred Bernica Blanton. Westmoreland, is a member of St Simmon's Episcopal Church and sits on the board of the Municipal Finance offices of the United States & Canada. Treasurer of the Ohio Valley Chapter of NAHRO and has served as a delegate for the National Society of Public Accountants in Montreal, Canada. Westmoreland, severed nine years as a member of the Planning Commission and ultimately as coordinator of basic planning for the city's Urban Renewal Program. His civic activities include : Active member of the Double V-Club, organizer of the Lincoln Heights Volunteer Fire Department, 1940, trustee of the Lincoln Heights Senior Citizens Club, Treasurer of the Black Elected Democrats of Ohio and Member of Lincoln Heights Voters League, to mention just a few. Westmoreland and his wife, who resides in Lincoln Heights are the proud parents of Carl Westmoreland and Guy T. Westmoreland Jr.

The Lincoln Heights Health Center board is pictured here. From left to right are (first row) Marylin Baughman, Lois ?, Reverend Walker, Nannie Scott, and Kathyrn Brown; (second row) Ethel Evans, Annie Rice, Roxie Foster, Charles Southall, Irene Joiner, Alonzo Wilkerson, and Delores Lindsay. (Courtesy of Angela Foster Thompson.)

Hodge Coal Company delivered coal in the community. However, Walker Ice Company was also a part of the business. (Courtesy of Mollie Mangham Spears.)

On stage at Lincoln Heights Elementary School, distinguished guests, such as Rev. Fred Shuttlesworth, Rev. Otis Moss, Steve Reece, and others, meet about the early civil rights movements. (Courtesy of Angela Foster Thompson.)

Former mayor of Cincinnati Theodore Barry and Rev. Ralph Abernathy were strong warriors for civil rights. Rev. James W. Jones was one of the freedom fighters along with others in the community for justice, equality, and civil rights. (Courtesy of Angela Foster Thompson.)

Singer, songwriter, and activist Isaac Hayes was here to help promote freedom, equality, and justice in the civil rights movement. (Courtesy of Angela Foster Thompson/Mount Moriah Baptist Church Archives.)

Here activist Hayes stands with the deejay from radio station WCIN, promoting equality for the community. (Courtesy of Angela Foster Thompson/Mount Moriah Baptist Church Archives.)

Five

SCHOOL DAYS

The first elementary school in Lincoln Heights was built in 1926 and was a part of the Woodlawn School District. Woodlawn Board of Education purchased 12.5 acres from Frank and Rose Medosch on the southern boarder of Grandview Heights on Magee Street and Lindy Street in Springfield Township. Nolte-Tillar Company built the school. The school was known as the Woodlawn Colony and was located on the corner of Steffens and Magee, which is the present site of the Lincoln Heights City Hall.

The Woodlawn Colony was a two-room portable building, which was assembled by James Hunter. The two teachers in the school were Laura Earhart and A. W. Bradford. The school grew, and five teachers were employed. In 1946, the city of Lincoln Heights came into incorporation. The school was a part of the Hamilton County School District.

In 1952, the South Woodlawn School came from Hamilton County to become an independent school district. The school was named Lincoln Heights Elementary School. The Lincoln Heights School Board, with Luther Lyle was the first president, appointed Theodore Malone as the first superintendent. Mary Lee, Robert Shively, James Simmons, and Frank Cannon served as principals during Malone's administration.

In 1957, the New Foundation Law handed down by the State Board of Ohio Education forced Lincoln Heights to make a decision to keep the Lincoln Heights City School System in tact by providing a high school for the pupils or to return to the county. Students were commuting to Lockland Wayne High School or other high schools in the Cincinnati Public School system after graduating from the Lincoln Heights Elementary School. The Cincinnati School Board said they could no longer accommodate Lincoln Heights's students because of their large numbers. The board and voters chose to build a high school, and in 1958, the Lincoln Heights High School was added to the system.

This class of 1950 picture was taken in front of Lincoln Heights Elementary School (formerly old South Woodlawn). (Courtesy of Richard Lewis.)

Here is the boys' side of the sixth-grade graduation at the old South Woodlawn School. From left to right are (first row) Lorenzo Leonard, Bob Johnson, Harold Dennis, Floyd Lightening, Tony Yates, unidentified, John Sharp, David Baxter, Hillman, Oneal Scott, and Lawrence Jones; (second row) Donald Matthews, unidentified, Sonny Price, Leroy downs, Herbert Dunigan, Tracy Freeman, unidentified, Billy Davis, Larry Wilson, and Benny Wagner; (third row) Clarence Gibbs, unidentified, Sonny Boggs, Donald Baynes, Marvin, Brown, Daniels, William, Johnson, and James Brady; (fourth row) Barnes, Best, Tommy Hunter, Ozman Mullis, Lloyd Mullen, Carl Ward, James Price, Eddie, and James. (Courtesy of Richard Lewis.)

South Woodlawn Public School's
commencement exercises program for the year
1950 is seen here. (Courtesy of Carolyn Carr.)

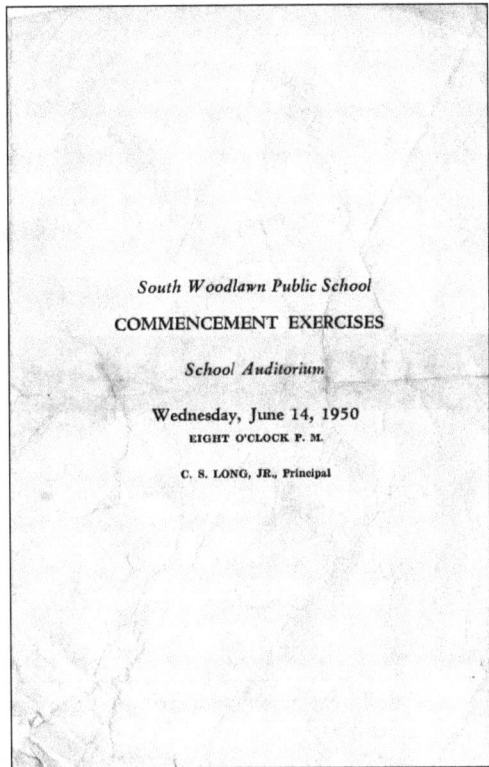

South Woodlawn Public School

COMMENCEMENT EXERCISES

School Auditorium

Wednesday, June 14, 1950
EIGHT O'CLOCK P. M.

C. S. LONG, JR., Principal

An unidentified family is
standing next to the old
elementary school. This area
is where Lincoln Heights High
School was built in the late 1950s.
In back of the family there is no
hill or sidewalk, which is present
today in the village next to the
elementary school. (Courtesy of
Marietta Roseman.)

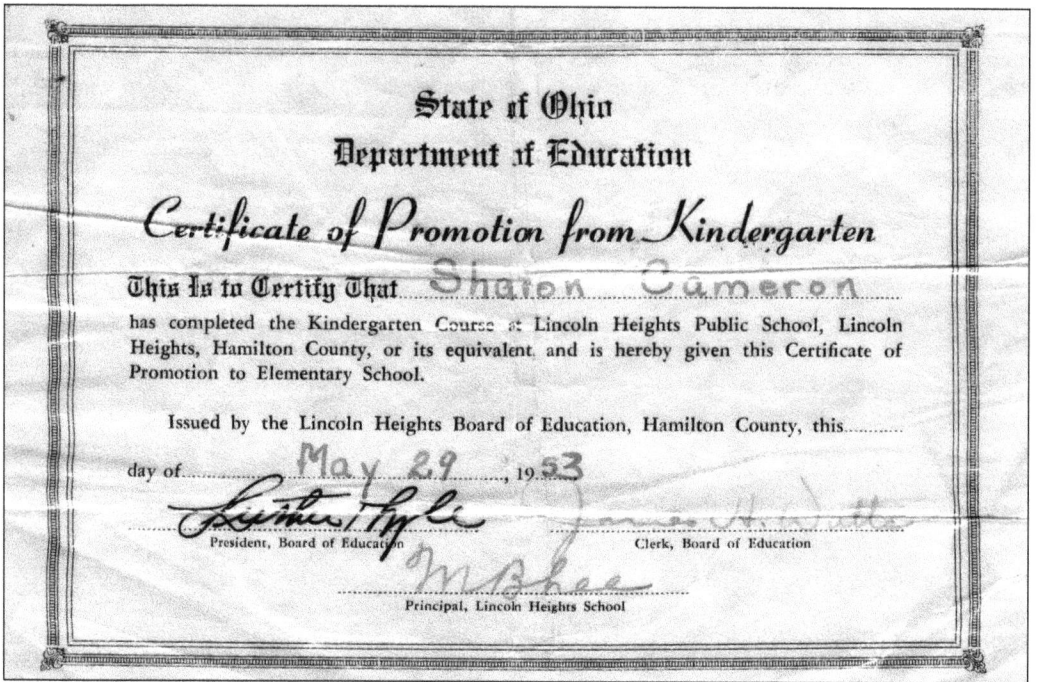

This certificate of promotion from kindergarten is for Deborah Cameron, issued by the Lincoln Heights Board of Education. President of the board was Luther Lye, and the principal of the school was M. Bhee. (Courtesy of Deborah Cameron.)

With Salley Isley on piano, students are on stage at the old South Woodlawn School building, which later became the Lincoln Heights Elementary School. Ron Isley is on the left side of the podium in the front row. (Courtesy of John Key.)

Students participate in the play *Wizard of Oz* in the old elementary school gymnasium. (Courtesy of Deborah Cameron.)

Here is the whole cast for the *Wizard of Oz* at the old elementary school. (Courtesy of Winfred Mangham.)

Students have a celebration in the elementary school gymnasium, listening to the music of the school band. It looks like a graduation. (Courtesy of Deborah Cameron.)

The band is playing at the celebration for the end of the year. Teachers Jake Zellars (left) and basketball coach John Hillard (right) are in the background. (Courtesy of Deborah Cameron.)

Here is the Ohio High School Athletic Association Southwestern District Class A Basketball Tournament at Princeton High School. Tournament time was the best time for the students and the school. Lincoln Heights consolidated with Princeton school district (Author's collection.)

**OHIO HIGH SCHOOL ATHLETIC ASSOC.
SOUTHWESTERN DISTRICT
CLASS A BASKETBALL TOURNAMENT**

PRINCETON HIGH SCHOOL

Chester and Sharon Roads
Cincinnati, Ohio 46
and

COLERAIN HIGH SCHOOL

**FEB. 17, 18, 24 &
MAR. 3, 4**

TOURNAMENT OFFICIALS

Robert Wolf, Tournament Manager
Tony Salvato, Assistant Manager

SOUTHWESTERN DISTRICT ATHLETIC BOARD

WILLIAM R. DODGE, *President*
EMERSON L. BROWN, *Vice President*
FRED L. DAFLER, *Secretary-Treasurer*
GUY E. SMITH
NELSON C. THINNES

Paul Landis, State Commissioner

FIRST ANNUAL ALL-SPORTS BANQUET

Sponsored by

City Recreation

School Board

Neighborhood Services

Saturday, April 23, 1966

Lincoln Heights Elementary Cafeteria

6:30 p.m.

This is the first annual All Sports Banquet held at Lincoln Heights Elementary School cafeteria. Lincoln Heights School District won several championships during its existence. The school district started with the class of 1959 and ended with the class of 1970. (Author's collection.)

The Lincoln Heights High School championship basketball team of 1970 poses here. Lincoln Heights won the championships for basketball, baseball, and football all in the same year. From left to right are (first row) Marty Seay, Greg Smith, Joe Key, Gregory Stemrick, Darryl Price, and Othel Rivers; (second row) coach Luther Greene, Rodney Whipple, Michael Lackey, Wendy Holloway, Greg Reese, ? Toran, ? Lee, unidentified, and coach John Hillard. (Courtesy of Carol Murden.)

This is an invitation to the junior-senior prom. The prom was held in the gymnasium with the juniors giving the seniors the prom. A prom committee was selected, and students worked a full year in order to achieve their goal of giving the seniors one of the best memories of the year. (Author's collection.)

L H S

The Junior Class of
Lincoln Heights High School
requests the pleasure of
your company at the
Junior-Senior Prom
on Friday, April twenty-eighth
nineteen hundred and sixty-seven
at nine o'clock in the evening
High School Gymnasium

R.s.v.p.

Ronald Smith

The Senior Class
of
Lincoln Heights High School
announces its
Commencement Exercises
Wednesday evening, May twenty-seventh
Nineteen hundred and sixty-four
six-thirty o'clock
High School Auditorium

BACCALAUREATE SERVICE
SUNDAY, MAY 24TH, 3:30 P. M.
EBENEZER SECOND BAPTIST CHURCH

Here is an invitation to the commencement for the 1964 graduating class of Lincoln Heights High School from senior Ronald Smith. (Author's collection.)

The Lincoln Heights High School talent show was one of the main attractions for the students at the school to show how gifted they were in singing, dancing, and musical ability. Here are Lorretta Shackleford and Eddie Whitehead on stage in the Lincoln Heights High School gymnasium doing a duet. This couple won the talent show on the Harry Rosedale Talent Hour Television Show on Channel 9. (Courtesy of Angela Foster Thompson.)

Here the Lincoln Heights High School band is playing for the talent show in the high school gymnasium. They are lead by James V. Roach, the music teacher. (Courtesy of Angela Foster Thompson.)

Danny Thomas is singing a solo in the talent show at Lincoln Heights High School. (Courtesy of Angela Foster Thompson.)

This male singing group of, from left to right, Dan Brock, Herbert Robinson, unidentified, Ruben Wilson, and unidentified came to the microphone with the same shirts and cummerbunds around their waists. They wanted to look the part and sing into the judges' hearts to win the contest. (Courtesy of Angela Foster Thompson.)

A band called the Rockin Rollers is trying to win the contest. It seems that this group is having a good time showing their talents to win this contest. (Courtesy of Angela Foster Thompson.)

Sitting in the classroom and having fun are Dorothy Pickens, Janet Clark, Diane Combs, Jackie Bailey, and Henrietta Overstreet. (Courtesy of Angela Foster Thompson.)

Hail, hail, the gang is all here. From left to right are (first row) Billy Turner, Tommy Perry, Sylvia Brady, Delores Brown, Lawrence Gore, and Jake McGee; (second row) Mabel Harris, Willa Crossity, Barbara Jones, and Dorothy Pickens. (Courtesy of Angela Foster Thompson.)

Posing for the camera after school are Betty Gales, Betty Franklin, Evonne Sweeney, Luke Anderson, and Pat Burton. (Courtesy of Angela Foster Thompson.)

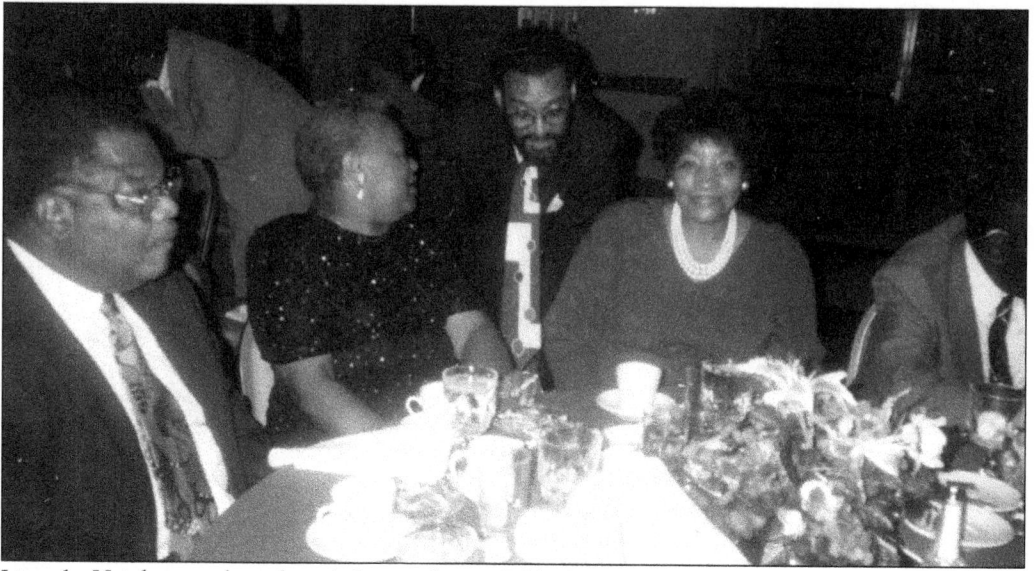

Lincoln Heights teachers from left to right are Eddie L. Starr, former Lincoln Heights principal; Mae Faggs Starr, former Olympic star; unidentified; and Mrs. McCullum. Mae Faggs Starr earned the distinction of being the first United States female to participate in three different Olympics (1948, 1952, and 1956). She won a gold medal in the 4-by-100-meter relay in at the 1952 games in Helsinki. A member of the Amateur Athletic Union (AAU) All-American women's track and field team from 1954 to 1956, she won the AAU 200-meter dash in 1954, 1955, and 1956. (Author's collection.)

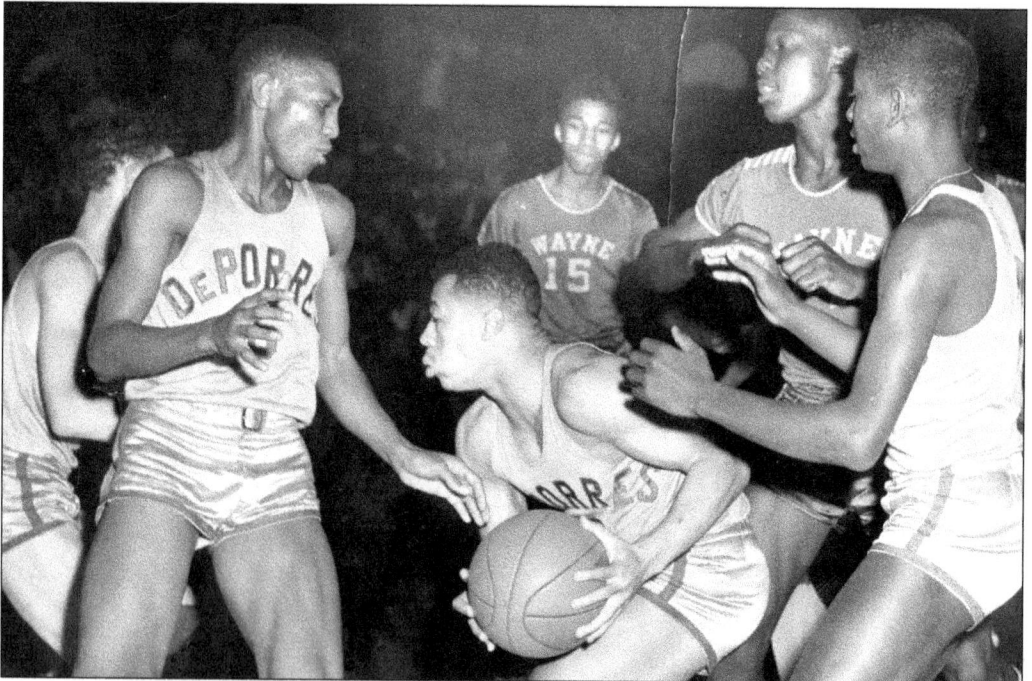

Here are members of the championship class B finals of Lockland Wayne School. Several members of the team lived in Lincoln Heights, including Richard Lewis, Richard Ellison (with the ball), Kendall Barnes, and Sam Wagner. (Courtesy of Richard Lewis.)

Seven

FOOD, FUN, AND FAMILY

The people of Lincoln Heights love their community. Every year, the Lincoln Heights Day Festival is the highlight of this small community, with booths for food, music, playing, rides, a soapbox derby, fireworks, the Miss Lincoln Heights Day pageant, and the Lincoln Heights Day Festival parade. Members of the community, old and young, line themselves along the parade route to enjoy this event. Former residents return just to enjoy this wonderful event-filled weekend, with family, friends, and memories. This festival represents the incorporation of the community. The city's chamber of commerce was the only charter ever granted by a national chamber of commerce to a group of African Americans.

As the festival approached, these are some of the signs that the summer is slowly coming to an end, and the children will be returning to school. Lincoln Heights's school days included fun activities such as basketball, football, baseball, jabberwocky, cheerleading, and yearbook club. The Lincoln Heights High School Tigers, wearing royal blue and gold, captured three sports event titles in one school year. The spirit of the community along with the school is a part of what has made Lincoln Heights what it is today.

This is the field where festival activities were held before the high school was built on Lindy Street. (Courtesy of Adrienne Howard.)

Here is the field where an all-night pig roast was held to raise money for a fire truck. Eventually, Lincoln Heights High School was built on this site. (Courtesy of Adrienne Howard.)

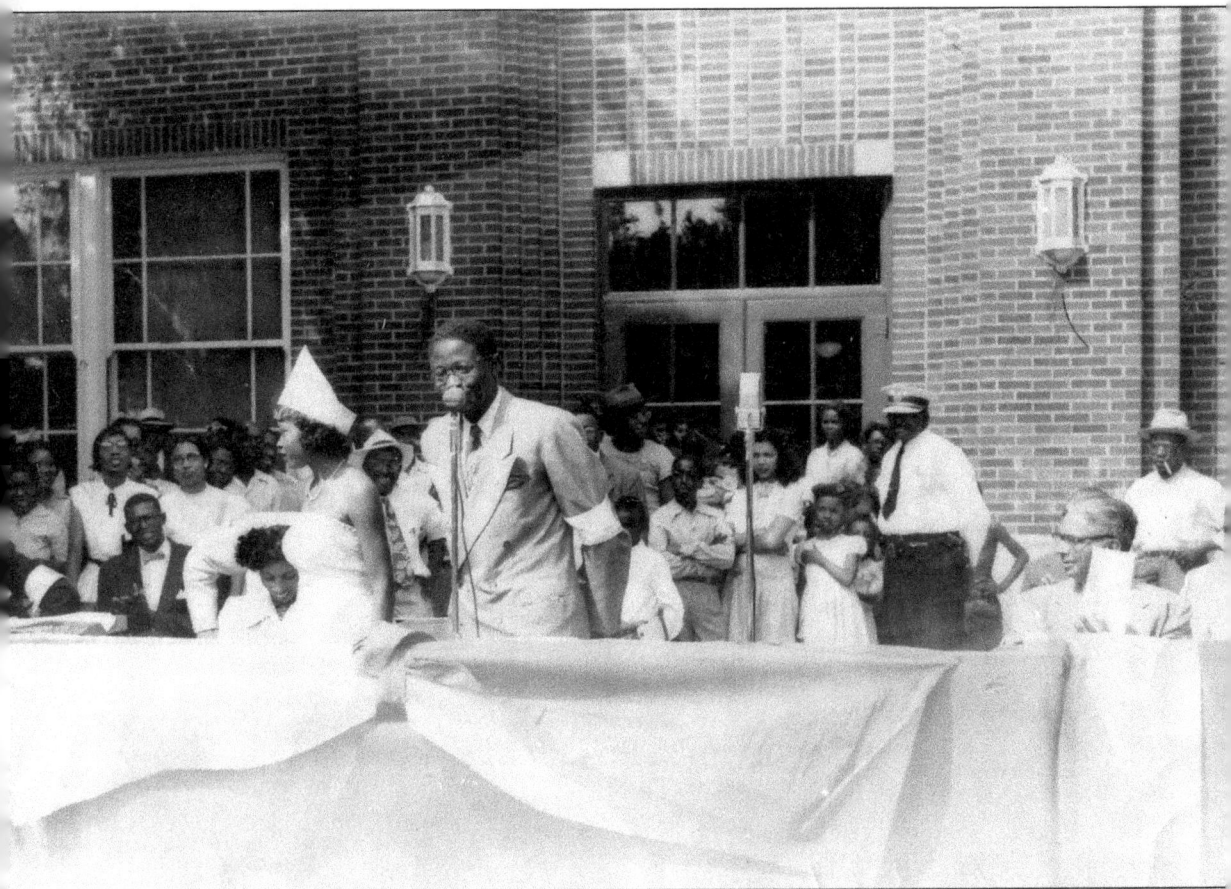

Alice Lindsay Larkins was crowned the first Miss Lincoln Heights on September 3, 1951, in front of the old South Woodlawn School and is seen here with village official Mayor Arthur T. Shivers. The most tickets sold won the title of Miss Lincoln Heights. (Courtesy of Mildred Lindsay Williams.)

Here is Miss Lincoln Heights and her court in the Lincoln Heights Day Festival parade. From left to right are Doris Holiday, Hortense Brewton (Miss Lincoln Heights), and Ethel May Shaw. (Courtesy of Mildred Lindsay Williams.)

The Miss Lincoln Heights Fire
Department honor was bestowed
upon Patricia Perry McDowell by
the Lincoln Heights Volunteer Fire
Department in 1957. (Courtesy of
Patricia McDowell.)

Cars line up along Leggett Street on the route for the festival parade. (Courtesy of
Adrienne Howard.)

Here is Mr. Caroll and his most decorative wagon in the Lincoln Heights Day Festival parade. He was the area garden tiller and ragman for the community. (Courtesy of Winfred Mangham.)

Unidentified members of the Valley Homes get their car together for the Lincoln Heights Day Festival parade. (Courtesy of Andrienne Howard.)

Excitement is in the air about decorating the car for the parade. Friends, family, and community come together for this event. (Courtesy of Adrienne Howard.)

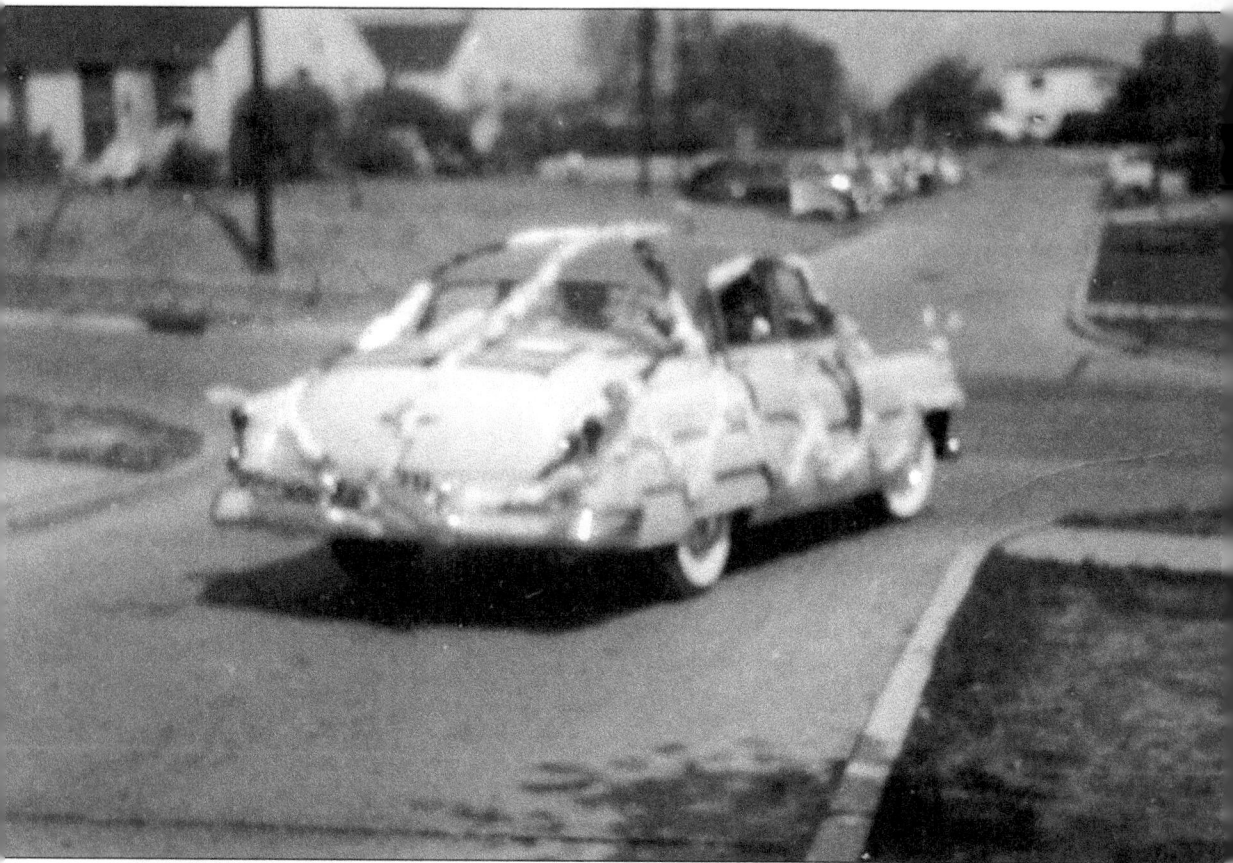

This decorative car is one of many that will participate in the Lincoln Heights Day Festival parade. (Courtesy of Adrienne Howard.)

Lincoln Heights Volunteer Fire Department always participates in the parade. It is one of the highlights of the village to see the men in their finest. (Courtesy of Winfred Mangham.)

The Lincoln Heights Volunteer Fire Department is one of the finest departments in the village. (Courtesy of Winfred Mangham.)

Here the firemen are participating in the parade down Leggett Street with truck No. 2. (Courtesy of Winfred Mangham.)

This is one of Lincoln Heights's first fire trucks in the Lincoln Heights Day Festival parade. Members of the volunteer fire department participate. (Courtesy of Winfred Mangham.)

Here spectators are lined up along the route enjoying the Lincoln Heights Day Festival parade moving down Leggett Street through the Valley Homes. (Courtesy Winfred Mangham.)

Here the young bikers of the Lincoln Heights Day Festival parade are riding along the route, showing their pride and their skills. (Courtesy of Winfred Mangham.)

These men are getting ready to participate in the Lincoln Heights Day Festival activities. (Courtesy of Winfred Mangham.)

This convertible car was used in the route for Lincoln Heights Day Festival parade. (Courtesy of Winfred Mangham.)

The General Electric Company was one of the sponsors for the fifth annual Lincoln Heights Day Festival celebration. Here are three unidentified young ladies on the truck float. (Courtesy of Marietta Roseman.)

Eight

PEOPLE OF

LINCOLN HEIGHTS

The youths of Lincoln Heights come from a long line of first families, such as the Goochs, Wootens, Satterwhites, Lewises, Lackeys, Lindsays, Woodruffs, Hunters, Moxleys, Danielses, Roziers, Shiverses Williamses, Kilgores, Lackeys, Flowerses, Finchers, Turners, Bradys, Perrys, Haskings, Wards, Moores, Richardsons, Taylors, Pattons, Summerors, Wynns, Smileys, Smiths, Bells, Kendricks, Smiltys, Boggses, Wavers, Danielses, Barnettes, Friersons, Brutons, Whiteheads, Lawsons, Craigs, Rices, Holloways, Westmorelands, Foldses, and others whose names may have been forgotten. From these families, the stars of future generations have shone ever so brightly.

There are many people from Lincoln Heights who have established themselves in the world today. People such as Nikki Giovanni, poet and educator; Charles Powell, certified public accountant; Clyde Brown; Charles Folds and Charles Spurling for the field of music; Hari Rhodes, actor; Anthony Yates; John Evans; Carl Westmoreland; Willis Holloway; William Dupree; Robbie Johnson, educator; Dr. Fred Bronson; Ethel Shaw, poet; Rev. Damon Lynch; Charles Whitehead; Alvin McCurdy, plant manager; and Deborah Clarke Wilhite, television. These individuals have inspired others to work hard toward their goals and even harder when they come upon obstacles that may appear to be unconquerable. They have encouraged the youth of Lincoln Heights to set goals high, to reach for the unattainable, to replenish or repossess their self-pride, and to have courage and determination within their inner being.

Anna Perry and her father, Frank Perry Sr., pose in front of their house on Byrd Street, which was named after Mr. Byrd of the community. (Author's collection.)

Here are Claude Perry, Francis Perry, and William Perry, father of Claude Perry. (Author's collection.)

From left to right, (first row) Sandra Whitehead and Carolyn Davis; (second row) Frank Perry, Treva Perry, and unidentified stand in front of the house on Byrd Street. (Author's collection.)

Robert Flowers and his wife pose in front of the house. (Courtesy of Winfred Mangham.)

Howard family members sit on the porch in one of the early family houses of Lincoln Heights. (Courtesy of Adrienne Howard.)

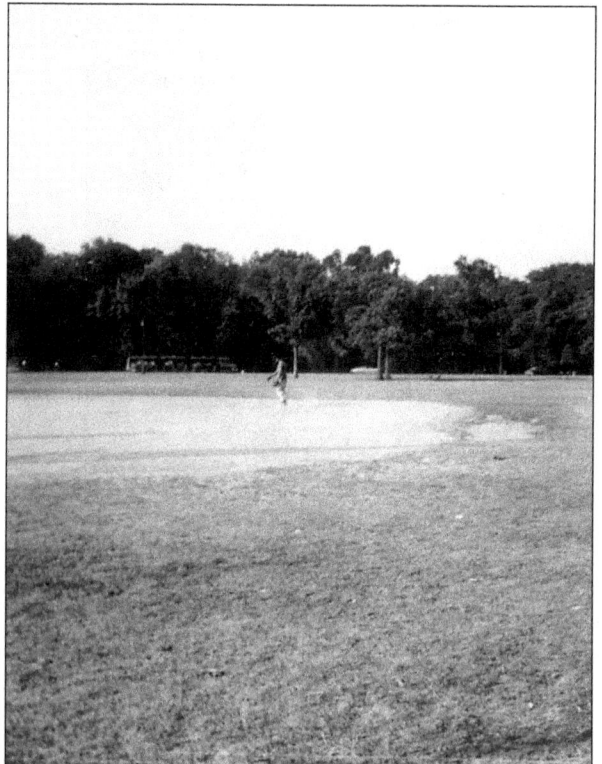

An unidentified person in the village plays ball on the only field. This field is the area where eventually the high school was built for the community of Lincoln Heights. (Courtesy of Adrienne Howard.)

The Ladies Auxiliary Club helped the community through any functions needed. Identified here are Geneva Mackey, Delores Mackey, Anna Jenkins, Dora Moxley, Lottie Jones, and Mattie Thomas Walker. (Courtesy of Mildred Lindsay Williams.)

The Lincoln Heights Women Civic Group president was Magnolia Craig, the wife of council member Luke Craig. Magnolia Drive is named for her. (Courtesy of Mildred Lindsay Williams.)

Lincoln Heights Community Club of 1951 was one of a few groups that helped to push for incorporation as well as help the community to grow. (Courtesy of Mildred Lindsay Williams.)

These ladies pose under the tree in the field of Lincoln Heights. Pictured are Mildred Lindsay, Patsy Satterwhite, Mrs. Thomas, Miss Purdue, and Mr. Smith's sister. (Courtesy of Andrienne Howard.)

Frank Perry of Lincoln Heights was the 1953 national AAU boxing champion in the 175-pound class. (Courtesy of Patricia McDowell.)

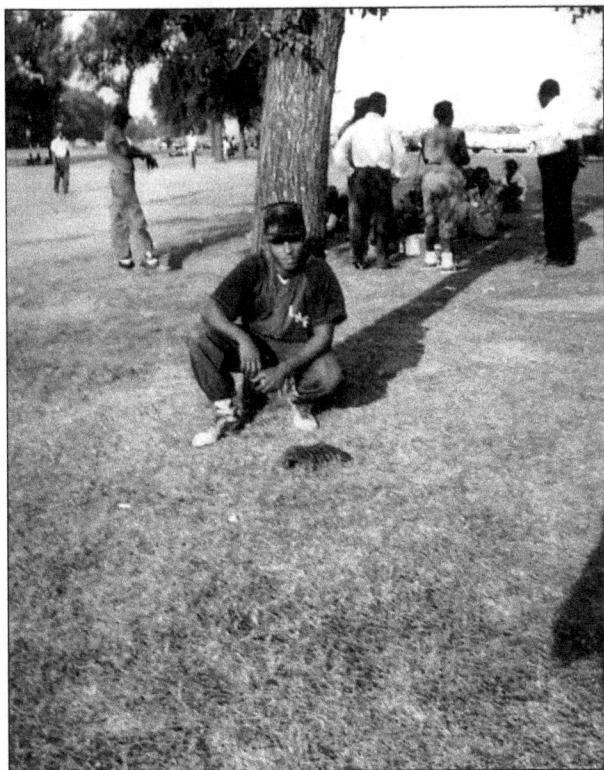

Dr. Sam Wilson was a member of the Lincoln Heights Fire Department's baseball team. (Courtesy of Adrienne Howard.)

Don Ellis was a member of the Lincoln Heights Fire Department baseball team. Games are played every year for the enjoyment and fun in the community. (Courtesy of Andrienne Howard.)

The Lockland Leaders girls' softball team was Hamilton County champions in 1950, 1951, and 1952 and was runner up in 1953. Pictured are, from left to right, (first row) Barbara Lindsay, Dorothy White, Virginia Matthews, Gwendolyn Matthews, and Jonnie Lee Rabb; (second row) Juanita Talbert, Peggy Bronston, Lillian Page, Elise Johnson, and Mattie Fryson; (third row) Treva Perry, Janice Johnson, Rosetta Smith, unidentified, Iva Price, Betty Barnett, Essie Mae Talbert, and coach R. Lindsay. (Courtesy of Mildred Lindsay Williams.)

The General Electric plant baseball team won the championship in 1953. Pictured are (first row) Mitchell Cobb, Milton Green, ? Bailey, Melvin Hayes, and Sam Ray; (second row) ? Brown, Rudy Singelton, Elbert Daniels, Evans Fitzgerald, Mac Ralls, James Matthews, and Bill Mitchell. (Courtesy of Mildred Lindsay Williams.)

Some of these men from the General Electric plant in the early 1950s were from Lincoln Heights. Mayor Arthur T. Shivers is standing on the far right in the white coat. Mr. Wolfork is fourth from the right, and Mr. Lackey is fourth standing on the left. These gentlemen were some of the first to have employment in a plant that made the B-29 bomber for World War II. (Courtesy of Mildred Lindsay Williams.)

From left to right, Ron Isley, Jimmy Hendrix, and O'Kelly Isley are featured in this photograph taken in the Atlantic Studio in 1965. Hendrix played in the Isley Brother's band before going solo. The Isley Brothers grew up in Lincoln Heights. They lived in the Valley Homes, and their mother was the pianist for Mount Moriah Baptist Church. (Courtesy of Frank Seay.)

From left to right (first row) unidentified and Ron Isley; (second row) unifentified, O'Kelly Isley, Ron Isley, Rudolph Isley, and Jimmy Hendrix were Grammy-winning recording artists. The Isley Brothers began as a quartet, but younger brother Vernon was killed in an automobile crash, leaving lead singer Ron and backup vocalists Rudolph and O'Kelly. When the Isleys sang, it moved people to tears. Whether they were harmonizing on a street corner, singing in church, or signing at a talent show, people packed the place to hear them. (Courtesy of Frank Seay.)

Actor Hari Rhodes played in the television series *Daktari* about an African game warden. Before going to Hollywood, he lived in the Valley Homes with his stepfather "Tank" Bonner. From left to right are Rhodes's sister Vivan Bonner; Rhodes; his wife; his mother, Bessie Bonner; and his stepfather Robert C. Bonner, whose nickname was "Tank." He was an employee of the Valley Homes. (Courtesy of Mildred Lindsay.)

From left to right, Benny Wallace, Allen Harrison Jr., Ben Massey, James Neal, and Luther "Step" Reese were another singing group. God placed a calling in the hearts of and an anointing on the voices of a group of bold gentlemen who he entrusted to take his word and minister in song. These men were obedient to the Holy Spirit and acknowledged their calling. They sang the Lord's praises under the name of Voices of Love. (Courtesy of Allen Harrison.)

From left to right are (first row) Roy Ford and Wash Hobson; (second row) Luther Leroy Reese, Allen Harrison Jr., James Neal, and Fletcher Cole. The Voices of Love group changed its name to the Gospelaires in the early 1950s. The name was chosen as a proclamation of the group's dedication to spreading the good news of the Lord and savior, Jesus Christ. (Courtesy of Allen Harrison.)

From top to bottom, Albert Washington, Fletcher Cole, Allen Harrison, James Neal, Ben Massey, and Luther Step Reese are seen here in late 1950s. They recorded under the Avant label, which was a sublabel of the Peacock Recording Company in Houston, Texas. During this time, they found out that the Gospelaires of Dayton were already recording at the Avant label using this name. The group underwent another name change. This time it was the Religious Gospelaires of Lincoln Heights. (Courtesy of Allen Harrison.)

Here, from left to right, are the members of the Gospelaires of Lincoln Heights, including Gerald Milton, Massey, James Taylor, Harrison, Benny Wallace, and Neal (seated). The group recorded their first 45 records in 1958. Peacock Records was prepared to give the group a recording contract. The group decided not to get into a binding agreement with anyone. (Courtesy of Allen Harrison.)

Lindy Street Baptist Church invited everyone to its picnic. From left to right are (first row) Fitzpatrick, Patricia Perry, Ida Mae Seay, four unidentified, and Curtis Nixon; (second row) unidentified, Donald Fitzpatrick, Albert Seay, M. Fitzpatrick, Derrick Fitzpatrick, Beatrice Ward, Anna Perry, Treva Perry, Ersntine Ford, unidentified, and Dorothy Hamilton; (third row) Mr. Williams, Mrs. Williams, Mrs. Fitzpatrick, unidentified, Randall Bridgeman, Willa Bridgeman, Mrs. Laura Ward, unidentified, and unidentified. (Courtesy of Patricia McDowell.)

They were called the Chamberlain Street gang, a group of children that lived on Chamberlain Street in Lincoln Heights. From left to right are (first row) Leonard Frierson, Grant Frederick, unidentified, and Carole Hope; (second row) Ida Mae Seay, Mattie Frierson, unidentified, Mattie Bell Fredericks, unidentified, unidentified, Albert Seay, and Hebert Whipple. (Courtesy of Albert Seay.)

Quincy Perry Davis graduated from Woodward High School at the age of 16. She was from Lincoln Heights. She was one of the first African American females in the state of Ohio to graduate from a physician assistant program. (Author's collection.)

These lovely ladies from Lincoln Heights, Venetta Lynch (left) and Patricia Perry, were posing for the camera on the steps of Central High School. (Courtesy Patricia McDowell.)

Anna Perry poses at the Castleform Ballroom. Perry was a strong advocate for education and children. The Anna B. Perry Seeds of Hope Scholarship Fund in Lincoln Heights has been created in her honor. Perry was a teacher for the Cincinnati Public School System. She was a lifelong resident of Lincoln Heights. (Courtesy Patricia McDowell.)

BIBLIOGRAPHY

Bureau of Educational Field Services, "Lincoln Heights Its People Its Schools Its Future." Miami University, Oxford, OH.

Mt. Moriah Baptist Church, "Lincoln Heights." Unpublished history of Lincoln Heights, OH.

Harrison, Allen. "History of Gospelairs." Lincoln Heights, OH.

Smith Maria Henrietta. "Black Suburbia Versus the Stereotype of Suburbia the History of Lincoln Heights, Ohio."

Taylor Louis Henry. "The Building of a Black Industrial Suburb: The Lincoln Heights Ohio Story." Ann Arbor Michigan: University Microfilms International.

Westmoreland Carl. "Lincoln Heights." Lincoln Heights, OH.

Westmoreland, Guy. "History of Lincoln Heights." Lincoln Heights, OH.

Visit us at
arcadiapublishing.com

....

www.ingramcontent.com/pod-product-compliance
Lightning Source LLC
Chambersburg PA
CBHW050648110426
42813CB00007B/1949